Incantation, Wendy

Incantation, Wendy

Frances Scott

Edited by
Beth Bramich

Bobo

Contents

7   *Introduction (Timesteps)*
     Mat Jenner

11 *Channels*
     Beth Bramich and Frances Scott
     with Chu-Li Shewring

29 *Becoming Human:*
     A Clockwork Orange, The Human League
     and Gender Liberation
     Juliet Jacques

41 *Valentina*
     Frances Scott

59 *Wendy, eclipsing*
     Stine Hebert

69 *Their waving signals a moon*
     Dave Tompkins

89 *rehearsal letter*
     Tom Richards with Frances Scott

99   Contributors
102 Image credits
103 Acknowledgements

Title pages throughout: film stills of Frances Scott, *Diviner*, 2017

---------- Forwarded message ---------
From: Mat Jenner <mj@taco.org.uk>
Date: Thu, 7 Jan 2021 at 20:44
Subject: Timesteps
To: F S <frances@abyme.org.uk>

Hey Frances,

Thanks for the update. No worries my end ofc. And sitting with the book title is a good idea.

How did it go with Tom, the filming and re-interpretation of 'Timesteps'? Good luck with the editing! You're always welcome to use TACO! for production whenever you need.

I somehow don't remember hearing 'Timesteps' when I watched *A Clockwork Orange*, but I like its time travelling connotations. Aside from the film, it seems like an apt theme tune for Thamesmead — enigmatic, moody, baroque, which suits the estate, don't you think? Thamesmead's nickname was *The Town Of Tomorrow* and that's how the GLC sold the town in promotional films in the 70s. I guess the grand Modernist vision of its architecture really did feel like the future at the time. I know people living here used to use the name ironically. It's since been adopted as part of Thamesmead's 're-branding'.

It's a good name though. I think you can place Thamesmead in a lineage of progressive ideas of the 'future'. Maybe that's what Kubrick picked up on when he chose it as a set for the film. The town, representing an attempt to build a future society in the present — a great social experiment, etc. Such a claim is always going to be pretty ripe for a take-down!

Since I've been working here, I've felt Thamesmead occupying multiple temporal spaces. Simultaneously in the past and the present, but with a foot planted in a near future. It's like it's haunted by a nostalgia for an idea of the future? Yet it's also being regenerated, so even now, the way it's talked about and understood is pregnant with a 'soon to be arriving tomorrow'. Maybe that's true of all places that are being developed, but I think that feeling is really pronounced here, and is somehow part of its fabric.

Architectural blueprint of build 'Stage 1', Thamesmead, London, 1968

It's been nearly 4 years since we started talking about *Wendy*! All starting with our walks around the estates and marshes. So many parts of the original Thamesmead have been pulled down in this time. It is especially sad that Binsey Walk has gone, so lucky that you managed to get onto the site the day before. I guess the demolition is a perfect analogy of the state of other progressive ideas right now. I don't think it's a coincidence that brutalist buildings across the UK are disappearing at this time. Maybe your project speaks to — or searches for — those progressive ideas? Just a thought.

Anyway, good luck with screening *Valentina* and the studio session at transmediale. Really looking forward to seeing it.

More walks soon,
Mx

Mat Jenner, TACO!
Excuse any mistakes - sent while mobile :-)

Channels

Beth Bramich and Frances Scott
with Chu-Li Shewring

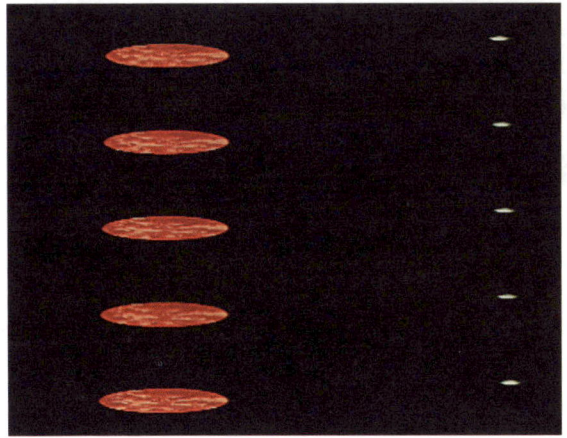

Accompanied by Wendy Carlos, Rachel Elkind,
Barbara Hepworth and Roshanak Kheshti

The following combines edited transcripts of conversations that took place from November 2020 to April 2021 at TACO!, London; at transmediale x CTM, Berlin; and on a video call between London and the Isle of Wight.

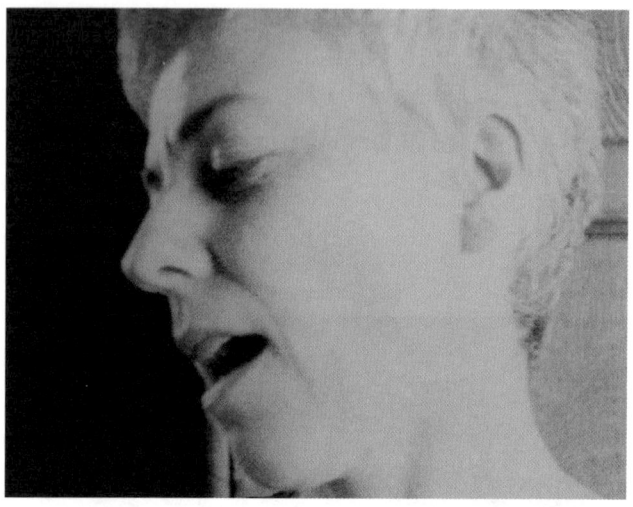

Beth Bramich   I thought we could start, Frances, by talking about your short film *Valentina* (2020). We see a performer, Valentina Formenti, and hear her recalling the transcript of an interview with Wendy Carlos, but the visuals and audio are out of sync.

Frances Scott   There's a disjunct between image and sound which came through the process of making the film. Towards the end of 1978, Wendy Carlos gave a series of recorded interviews with journalist and gay liberation activist Arthur Bell for an article in *Playboy* magazine. There were more than 800 manuscript pages from their conversations, but they were edited into a much shorter piece that, in the end, homed in on Carlos's transition. Maybe Arthur Bell was writing to who he thought was the readership, or maybe the magazine exercised editorial control, because his voice is annexed after the introduction – it's 'Playboy' as interviewer. Wendy is very tolerant in the way she handles the questions, but the final edited interview is reductive, missing much of what Bell dismisses as 'cosmic ramblings'. It skims over her career as a composer and her practice in other fields, like solar eclipse photography. She is a polymath, an innovator, a self-confessed 'Coronaphile'! It might seem strange now to think of

Film still of Frances Scott, *Valentina*, 2020

Playboy as a radical publication, but I guess it was seen as having a more progressive agenda then. I think Wendy was disappointed with the interview's focus.

During my research, I came across two tape recordings of the interview in the Music Division of the New York Public Library. It was moving to encounter

Wendy's voice in that space – she's right there with you. There's always an intimacy with this kind of close listening in the archive. I became interested in the content that had been excluded, the missing aspects of their conversations.

A few months later, I shot 100 feet of black-and-white 16mm film with Valentina Formenti. She read aloud, holding in her memory the sentences from the transcript and substituting some of the forgotten words with her movement. With a hand-wound Bolex camera you have a few seconds, maybe twenty or thirty with each mechanical wind, so the reading was pretty fragmented, even though 100 feet of film represents only about two and a half minutes. We didn't do an audio recording at the time, because the Bolex sounds like a sewing machine at full pelt! So, there's no sync sound. It was more of a rehearsal, to conjure Wendy's presence in her absence. In those first months of the pandemic lockdown, we returned to the rushes and recorded the reading online, using a phone mic mediated through intermittent internet connections. Valentina followed the arc of the silent film, lip-reading and lip-syncing to the image of herself, a double remembering. I also worked with sound designer Chu-Li Shewring, who processed Valentina's voice through a vocoder.

Beth Bramich   This could be a good place to talk about your collaboration with Chu-Li and how you have worked with her to explore Wendy's music?

Frances Scott   I've worked with Chu-Li on a number of projects. Early in my research, we made *Incantation, Wendy* (2018), which we thought of as a sort of magic spell or invocation. It was a 100-minute-long compilation of Wendy Carlos's records interspersed with recordings of our own that we broadcast on TACO!'s community radio station, RTM.FM. Chu-Li had also introduced me to Wendy Carlos's 1972 *Sonic Seasonings*, produced by Rachel Elkind. Each side of the LP is a season – spring, summer, winter, fall. There's a beautiful line on the album

Film still of Frances Scott, *Diviner*, 2017

cover, attributed to 'anonymous', that says: *I am moving all day and not moving at all. I am like the moon underneath the waves that ever go rolling.* I love this – the moon beneath the waves. What an image!

Rachel Elkind All this is to simply explain what *Sonic Seasonings* is all about: it is an aural tapestry, created by the imagination and expertise of Wendy Carlos, from impressionistic and expressionistic experiences of Nature. It contains natural sounds recorded in Quad as realistically as possible and subtly mixed with electronic and instrumental sounds in an effort to create four evolving, undulating cycles evocative of the moods of Earth's seasons. We have manipulated these sounds – electronically orchestrated them so to speak – into an amalgam of the natural and the synthetic.

This was on my mind when approaching Thamesmead, and what I saw as a blurred space between concrete walkways, underpasses, steps and the lake, and then the wildlife, bats at twilight, herds of horses in

Chu-Li Shewring If you hear the sound of a horse hoof normally, it occupies different tones and timbres. But when it's put through a vocoder, it's really reduced in a way – you hear one tone or multiple tones, like in a chord. It becomes musical, in a simplified,

Architect's collage showing proposal for lakeside dwellings with terraces, Thamesmead, London, 1966

marshland edging the estate and river. It became a set. And of course, it had been a film set, for Stanley Kubrick's *A Clockwork Orange* (1971). We introduced the horses into the radio session, and they sounded as if they were galloping towards the microphone.

One of the clips we used is from *Secrets of Synthesis*, an album Wendy released in 1987. She talks about her composition for 'Timesteps', one of the tracks in *A Clockwork Orange*, as a way of warming up to more synthesised vocals in Beethoven's Ninth Symphony. But what I remembered was her talking about vocoders being more useful when they're doing things that are 'not particularly vocal'.

```
stripped-down way that takes away
the recognisability of it. What's
interesting about the hooves is
that we're trained to understand
what that sound is, because we've
heard it before… I think what
really flips it is the breath at
the end. I mixed the horses by
reducing the vocoder, and then
you have the animal. You're not
a hundred per cent sure if it's
a horse. And it's strange, because
at the point you hear the breath,
you don't know if it's a human
or not.
```

```
Chu-Li     I was really playing with
Shewring   the pitches. Some parts
are so deep, they're so degraded,
you can't recognise the words.
They just become texture. The
textures become close to the
image, to the hand-processing.
So it seems to marry quite well,
in an uncanny way.
```

```
Wendy      My collaborator at the
Carlos     time, Rachel Elkind, and I
experienced our first success with
electronic voice synthesis. But
first, a little background. After
working on electronic simulations
of orchestral sounds, I thought,
why not try vocal sounds as well?
I soon learned that the most dis-
tinctive qualities of the human
voice are inherently much more
difficult to synthesise than seem-
ingly equally complex qualities of
instrumental sounds […] Remembering
Homer Dudley's invention of the
vocoder in the '30s, I asked Bob
Moog to put together something
like a vocoder, using his standard
modules. We originally called it a
Spectrum Encoder Decoder - what a
terrible name! Of course, vocoders
may be well known now, but they
were hardly on everyone's lips
in those days.
```

I really enjoy her talking us through her process. I guess this is as close as we can get to that.

Ogata Kôrin, *Matsushima zu byôbu* (*Waves at Matsushima*), 18th-century Japan. Six-panel folding screen. Original artwork used on Wendy Carlos's album *Sonic Seasonings* (CBS, 1972)

Beth Bramich   It's fantastic to hear Wendy's voice. You can hear her passion for her work and her sense of humour in the recording. Maybe we could talk about the soundtrack to *Valentina* and how the collaborations on sound and performance will feed into the long-form film *Wendy*, which you're currently working towards?

Frances Scott   The music you hear in *Valentina*, over the credits but also woven throughout, is by musician and instrument designer Tom Richards. In 2016 he built the Mini Oramics, based on an unrealised 1976 design by Daphne Oram. Tom worked from her plans. Oram is credited with inventing 'drawn sound synthesis', and the original Oramics is a musical interface that reads graphic scores, drawn by the composer. Oram used to draw her scores on 35mm film, which is something that appeals to me.

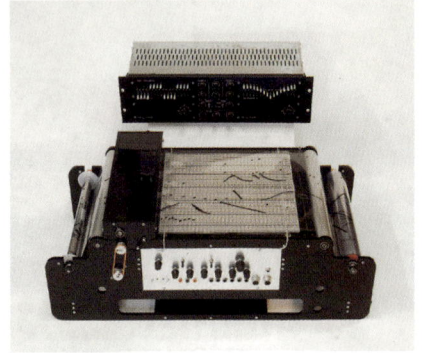

Tom interpreted Wendy Carlos's 'Theme from "A Clockwork Orange" (Beethovania)' (1971) – which is her riffing on Henry Purcell's 'Music for the Funeral of Queen Mary' in the style of Beethoven – and transcribed it for the Mini Oramics. What you hear in *Valentina* is the warm-up, a rehearsal for the rehearsal. Tom and I did an event with the scores-in-progress at TACO! in 2019, and at transmediale x CTM in Berlin in 2021. What often happens is that the material generated in rehearsals, or periods where I might not be scripting something, ends up in the work. For *Wendy*, Tom will transcribe and elaborate on these scores. It's a way of edging towards something, but you're always edging beyond it.

In *Valentina*, I edited the voices, the structure, and Chu-Li picked out incidental sounds, like a child's voice, or birds outside the window of Valentina's flat. Alongside synthesised, vocoded narration, there are moments of her natural voice in the space. Sometimes Valentina's talking but you can't hear anything.

Chu-Li Shewring   My favourite bit is where you can't hear anything! [*laughs*] But that only works because of everything else. There's something arresting about silence. I think I might have accidentally recorded my email-incoming sound too. I was getting the line-out of my computer into the vocoder, and when my email came in, it just obliterated a certain

Tom Richards, Mini Oramics, 2016

> word – it popped out. Because it was vocoded you
> didn't recognise that sound. We're not trying to
> understand it anymore, but we're enjoying it for the
> texture, or for the quality of it. We're disassociat-
> ing from language and words, moving towards sounds.
> At times like this we're looking at her movements,
> looking at her lips, and then it becomes quite alien…
> You feel like an alien looking at another alien,
> from another planet.

Beth Bramich   We've been speaking for some time about your research process and how you've approached exploring Wendy's life and work. Could you talk about your own process of synthesis and association, how it's allowed you to find a route through Wendy's work and archival material?

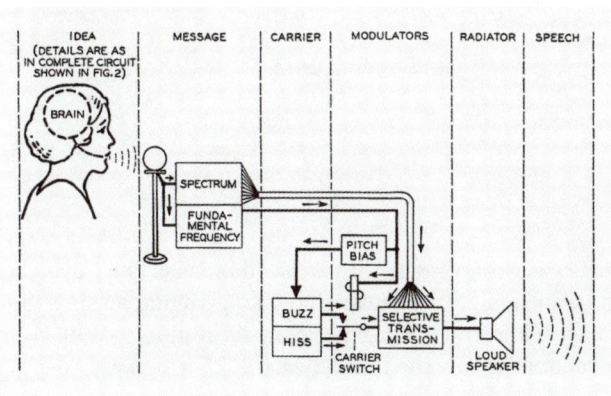

Frances Scott   I'm interested in the idea of synthesis, not as something 'synthetic', but in the origins of the word: to bring together elements that react and make something else. For me, synthesis is this idea of combining and recombining. In 2019, I made *PHX [X is for Xylonite]*, a film running at a tangent to and alongside my research for *Wendy*. In *PHX*, I was working with polymer chemists, and looking at the first plastics, which were semi-synthetic. Plastic is the ultimate union, really! Cellulose nitrate was used as the substrate for early film, beneath the gelatin layer, and I'd like to feature this in *Wendy* – to show the processes used in the conservation of film, where these layers are separated. I often bring together what might feel like disparate material or narratives that come through conversations or other kinds of research. I try to do this so that the materials create their own script, by brushing up next to each other, in a sort

Homer Dudley, vocoder schematic, 1940

of close dance. With *Wendy*, partly because of what is available, and also my desire to be sensitive to her presence in public space, this process of association has taken me to other places – interpreting the scores with Tom on the Mini Oramics, re-enacting occluded interview material, looking out for eclipses happening now. These will all feature. Roshanak Kheshti talks about synthesis in her brilliant book on Wendy's *Switched-On Bach* (1968), and refers to Wendy calling herself, the 'Original Synth':

> Roshanak Kheshti 'Original Synth' reveals through juxtaposition that origins are synthetic; they are artificial and manufactured-yet-necessary myths made real for the purposes of rationalising the present. Yet the phrase also subtly points to the original meaning of 'synthesise' – the deeply human act of creating new knowledge – revealing the contradictions inherent to a reading of electronic music as that which is artificial and in direct opposition to the 'natural' sounds of the acoustic. 'Original Synth' is also a pun, riffing on the Christian origin myth in which the desire for knowledge and the knowledge of desire – in the allegorical form of Eve's feminine sexuality – narratively function as Christian man's downfall.

I'm also working closely with artist-filmmaker Phil Coy to create environments using volumetric filmmaking, digital meshes that can carry images, such as the hand-processed 16mm footage. We're thinking about the way the film *TRON* (1982), which was also scored by Wendy, combined backlit film cells with computer animation, for example. These will become spaces that Valentina moves through.

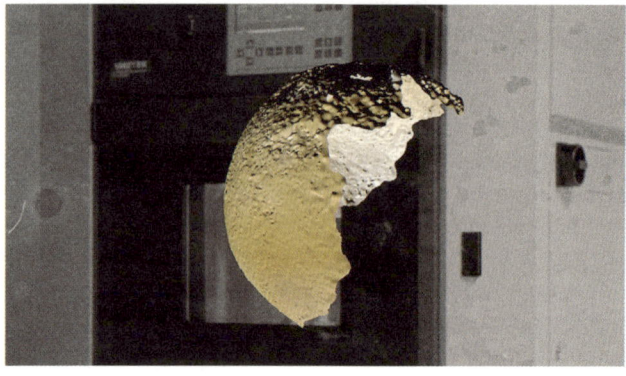

Film still of Frances Scott, *PHX [X is for Xylonite]*, 2019

Beth Bramich   This process of synthesis also relates to the drawing together of thoughts, ideas, information and other material. I want to ask about your approach to archives, what draws you to particular material, and whether you could speak about the kinds of subjective and instinctive connections you make through association. Perhaps this relates to your film *Diviner* (2017) and the journey you made through the South West Film & Television Archive (SWFTA, Plymouth) as well as to the way that Wendy's solar eclipse photography spoke to you?

Frances Scott   I'll start my research in a particular archive because it speaks to a project, and I have initial ideas about approaching the catalogue. But I'm more than open to distraction! The 'finds' you can't preempt are usually the interesting ones. Some of these are like pulses of light, they illuminate something else nearby. I wonder if this receptive state of being is like witnessing an eclipse – you're experiencing something total even though your perception is made from much smaller moments. Everything is changing around you, and you're changing too. Before I made *Diviner*, I'd seen a short documentary at SWFTA about a water dowser, and I was thinking about the diviner as a searching figure. Maybe it's also how I feel in these contexts, in seeking out connections. I had archive footage in mind, but I let myself be suggestible. The scoring material was the behind-the-scenes footage of cast and crew on films like Jerzy Skolimowski's *The Shout* (1978), which was shot in the South West. I wanted to suggest impossibility in the production, where everything is connected – poets, protests, paranormal activity, planets – and the landscape itself is a constantly evolving set.

    I'd originally wanted to make another work in the archive. Called *Last Suns*, it was going to be a series of photographic enlargements of bodies of light, taken from some of the film frames in *Diviner* – 'stilling' something in motion.

> **Barbara Hepworth**   I like to find some kind of eternal form, which in a thousand years, I could live with.

    Maybe this is why I'm drawn to Wendy's solar eclipse photographs. She made journeys, sometimes over great distances, to witness this incredible transition that happens regardless of whether we see it or not. She isolates that moment for us.

Film still of Frances Scott, *Diviner*, 2017

Beth Bramich   You've described your films *Valentina* and *Wendy* as 'speculative portraits', and also 'fan letters'. I'm really curious about what that opens up for you. You mentioned that Wendy took a step back as a public figure, and that she's also someone who experienced marginalisation during and as a consequence of her gender transition. Could we talk about how your film operates as a fan letter in this context?

Frances Scott   I think of *Wendy* and *Valentina* as fan letters because they're not films about Wendy Carlos. Wendy was critical of a recent biography, perhaps because it touches too closely on her personal life. But she's been open to those who respond to her music or her wider work. A fan letter allows me to think about her in orbit. She's there as a talisman or guide. I've almost had to try to create a proximity through distant means. I've spent a lot of time with her website, which is an archive in itself – complex and brilliantly weird in places, and difficult to navigate your way back from! She's generous, making resources available there, including scores or MIDI files. I see it as an online work.

I'm interested to find that same feeling, in *Wendy*, that you have in encountering her website. I want to express a sort of electric impulse, like synaptic connections, or transmissions between scenes, to suggest Wendy.

`Chu-Li Shewring   When you recognise something, you almost go with it in a comfortable way, but when you don't quite recognise something, it makes you lean in towards it.`

Beth Bramich   Looking through the material you've pointed me to, I feel a strong desire from Wendy not to be externally defined. This runs through her adoption of 'Original Synth', the steps she has taken to control where her music can be heard, and her returning to music she created for films – for example, the expanded edition she released in 1972, of the music she composed for *A Clockwork Orange*. She asserted her own authorship over what she produced for the film, including things that may seem peripheral to Kubrick's vision but are essential to her.

I was wondering how the film *Wendy* and this book, which will be published before the film is completed, will sit together? The commissioned essays will address some of Wendy's different interests that you found through your research and are still exploring as you develop the film.

Frances Scott The book-before-the-film might seem like a back-to-front way of producing, perhaps it's more usual to have a book about a film published alongside it or after its release. I want the book to feel like it's in-process, unmade and making itself as it goes. It becomes an abstract screenplay, articulating what's to come. How might the book shape the film? I was also drawn to Wendy's process of scoring 'Timesteps' in response to Anthony Burgess's novel, before she knew about Kubrick's film adaptation. This prelude appeals in the way it prioritises writing over image-making, but it's absolutely about making images! Our many conversations, Beth, and the commissioned essays by Stine Hebert, Juliet Jacques and Dave Tompkins, all speak to Wendy in different ways – through her fascination with eclipses, her influence on post-punk, her part in the history of gender liberation, or in her exploratory work with the vocoder and the synthesis of speech.

Beth Bramich The different ways you're trying to build a fuller picture of Wendy are not intended, I think, to be comprehensive or to define her and her career, but rather to pick up on what is less known or has been erased from the archives. You've already mentioned how Wendy's self-definition through her website is so significant to you.

In the different processes of researching and making the film, you've seemed to want to keep the sense you're getting of her as a person *live*. To follow on from that, could we talk more about how you're working with volumetric filming, and also the eclipse? *Valentina*, visually, has these very striking exposures – moments of intense, overwhelming light.

Frances Scott Those pulses and flares of light happened in hand-processing the film in the lab with Bea Haut. There's an instability or 'moving' of other forms within the frame, like ghosts. Scenes in *Wendy* will combine hand-processed film with volumetric filmmaking processes. Phil and I have been using custom software with a modified Xbox sensor as a depth camera, which captures space as a series of coordinates. It means that you can almost move through the image. For example, you can choose whether you want to view the figure front-on or from the side. Animation allows you to create spaces and people. In some ways, the possibilities of creating or

Film still of Frances Scott, *Diviner*, 2017

abstracting an eclipse through this other form of image-capture is inviting – how can we suggest a transition of celestial bodies without seeing it happen?

I'm also intrigued by the origin of the word 'eclipse'. In Greek it stems from 'abandonment' or 'disappearance'. There's a nice connection too with mythical animals that were believed to consume the sun or moon during an eclipse – wolves, frogs and toads. In China, where the earliest word for eclipse, *shih*, translates as 'eat', it was a dragon that bit into the sun. I watched the total solar eclipse visible in Argentina last year as a live stream, and I'm now working out how I can approach an annular solar eclipse that will be visible from northern Canada and Greenland this summer. Wendy captured every total solar eclipse between 1972 and 1985. Incredibly, she also developed photographic processes to composite images for a better exposure, and these have been published by NASA – quite a thing! This analogue, predigital technique speaks to me around ideas of material layering and synthesis, and of creating an experience that attempts to exceed the limitations of the body.

Beth Bramich Returning to this idea of the voice, I really loved what you wrote about your research project at an earlier stage, in a sort of mission statement published on TACO!'s website to 'explor[e] the synthesised, un-bounded voice across fields of music, literature and film'. The vocoder removes a lot of qualities that we might use to make assumptions about an individual. The idea of Wendy and her compositions moving 'un-bounded' across these worlds resonates for me with the voice becoming freer by its deconstruction or translation.

Volumetric film test made by Frances Scott and Phil Coy, March 2020

Photograph taken by Beth Bramich on a walk with Frances Scott, Greenwich, London, April 2021

When you speak about Wendy's film scores and collaborations, it really reminds me of your approach to filmmaking, particularly how you work with different people over these long periods of development. I was wondering if you have documented any of your conversations, particularly while working remotely due to the pandemic?

Frances Scott I was about to go 'No!' [*laughs*], but that's not entirely true.
It did happen in the process of making *Valentina*, unintentionally. The video-call lip-syncing was a necessary process, but it also became an expanded conversation between Valentina and me, and between Chu-Li and me, and that very simple gesture multiplied and drew us in together. In one of our email conversations, Dave Tompkins said that he thought our collaboration in the film was somehow the working parts of a speech mechanism, but using *the unsaid and unvoiced, as well as to 'say' it, to 'tell' it*. I'm paraphrasing him, but collaborating, between the channels of subconscious and voice, allows you to reach a kind of totality. That's a beautiful idea, and maybe not something I'd realised when we were in the midst of it, but it's something I'd like to take into *Wendy* – her and our multiple voices.

What was weird for me was not being able to work alongside Chu-Li during this period. Usually I send a rough cut ahead of time, and then we work quite intensely in her studio. She still received the cut, but with the audio from a phone recording!

Chu-Li Shewring *Valentina* was still a very intuitive process – we always work like this, don't we? There are no post-it notes all over the wall that we're trying to reorder. You're not thinking too much, you're reacting. It's immediate. I was looking at her and mixing it according to what she's saying or how she's moving. We might have tried a few more things if we'd been together, but maybe not. It's hard to know, because as an idea it's more simple than, say, *Diviner* (2017).

Valentina has become the document of the conversations, in speculative correspondence with Wendy, and in correspondence with those I work closely with – a collective telling. Maybe the vocoder is present, or the idea of it, even when it's not vocoding. And what we're doing now is another kind of document or translation of these

Film still of Frances Scott, *Diviner*, 2017

voices, recording this conversation to transcribe it, and potentially elements will appear in the book. I guess that's always part of my thinking – to capture material that might be useful later, moving beyond what's in front of you.

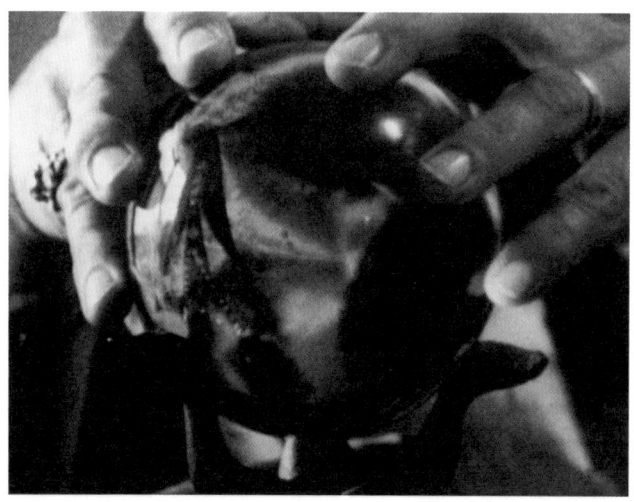

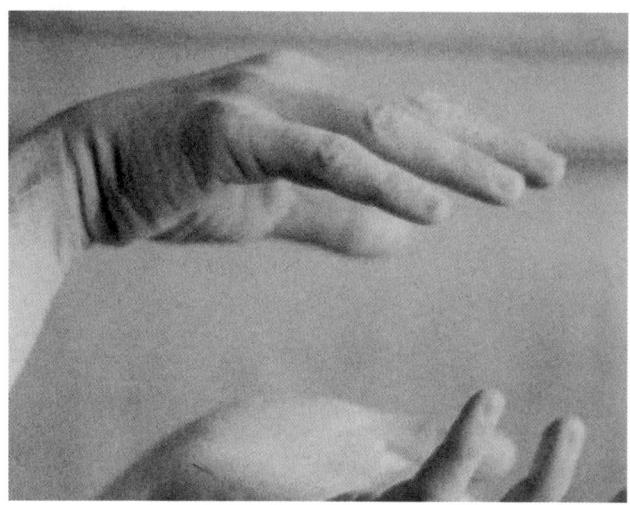

Film still of Frances Scott, *Diviner*, 2017   Film still of Frances Scott, *Valentina*, 2020

ACCOMPANIMENTS

Rachel Elkind, LP notes for Wendy Carlos, *Sonic Seasonings*,
A TEMPI Production for CBS Inc, 1972

Wendy Carlos, 'Vocal Synthesis', *Secrets of Synthesis*,
CBS Inc, 1987

Roshanak Kheshti, *Wendy Carlos's Switched-On Bach*
(33 1/3 series), New York and London: Bloomsbury Academic, 2019

Barbara Hepworth speaking in Frances Scott, *Diviner*, 2017

Becoming Human:
A Clockwork Orange,
The Human League and
Gender Liberation

Juliet Jacques

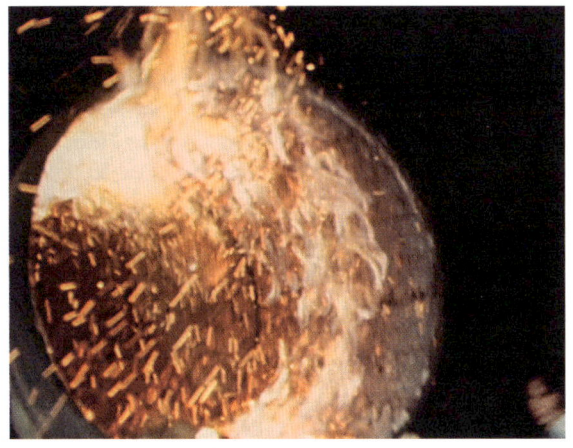

'The public turned out to be amazingly tolerant or, if you wish, indifferent', Wendy Carlos told *People* magazine in 1985, six years after coming out as transgender in an interview with *Playboy*. After the surprise success of *Switched-On Bach* in 1968 – made with producer Rachel Elkind, the album went on to win several Grammy Awards and sold more than a million copies within several years – Carlos spent the next decade hiding her transition for fear of losing work, friends and family. By coming out in *Playboy*, she hoped to stop feeling she had to conceal her identity to be able to work. In this, she paralleled British travel writer Jan Morris, who in 1974 published the memoir *Conundrum* to take control of the narrative around her transition even as she worried she would be defined as the 'Sex Change Author'. For Carlos, there was no public backlash, perhaps *because* she had been so reclusive. She explained to *People*, 'There had never been any need of this charade to have taken place. It had proven a monstrous waste of years of my life.'

That Carlos was so worried about the consequences at the time is quite understandable. The transsexual composer Angela Morley did not go public until five years after her gender confirmation surgery in 1972.[1] In the autobiography *Man Enough to be a Woman* (1995), named after one of her songs, transsexual punk musician Jayne County talks about how scenes that celebrated gender play and androgyny sidelined her once she began her transition. In response to artist, writer and technician Sandy Stone's work as a sound engineer with the all-women Olivia Records collective, Janice Raymond's book *The Transsexual Empire* (1979) argued that 'all transsexuals rape women's bodies by reducing the real female form to an artefact'.[2] But in the face of all this, why would *any* trans person – especially one who had unexpectedly achieved fame – keep quiet? (Even as they were often encouraged to do by the clinicians who handled their transitions.)

Since the 1980s, Carlos has largely declined to be interviewed and she has made it clear she doesn't want to be an advocate for any trans community. Like Sandy Stone, she was an early adopter of the internet, recognising that it would allow more control over her statements and their framing: the biography on her website does not mention her transition; a section 'On Prurient Matters' expresses her frustration at people who focus on her private life of fifty years ago.[3] Writing as a transsexual woman – albeit one who has extensively discussed the realities of such a life, hoping to liberate others from having to do so – I understand Carlos's boredom and irritation, which must only grow with age. Carlos is of interest, after all, due to her *compositions*. Rather than explore these through the prism of her personal life, I would like to focus on how her work has intersected with film and architecture to influence a generation of musicians who didn't yet know how she identified – and most likely would not have cared.

*

Specifically, I want to explore Carlos's influence on the British post-punk movement thanks to her popularisation of the Moog synthesiser with *Switched-On Bach* and her soundtrack for *A Clockwork Orange* (1971). That film captured the imagination of musicians – despite director Stanley Kubrick's request that it be withdrawn from UK circulation in 1973 after it was cited in trials for rape, manslaughter and murder. 'Post-punk' is a slippery term: I use it to mean music made between 1978 and 1982 by people who felt punk had opened doors for them but who wanted to make more musically and/or intellectually sophisticated work; these artists' use of synthesisers in particular set them apart from their predecessors. Various elements that the post-punk artists were interested in – post-war composition; pop music from the UK, the US and Germany; film, literature and architecture – all came together in *A Clockwork Orange*.

Histories of British post-punk, be it Simon Reynolds's *Rip It Up and Start Again*, published in 2005, or the BBC's *Synth Britannia* documentary, directed by Ben Whalley and broadcast in 2009, have Kubrick's film and Carlos's soundtrack at their core. Many post-punk musicians came from working-class or petit bourgeois backgrounds and post-industrial cities, and they noticed how *A Clockwork Orange* captured 'the desolate psychogeography of the new Britain created by the "visionary" town planners and fashionably Brutalist architects of the 1960s'.[4] J.G. Ballard's novels, especially *Crash* (1973), were their other great literary inspiration, for similar reasons. But really it was Kubrick's dystopian film that cemented these artists' connection to 'high-rise blocks, shadowy underpasses, concrete pedestrian bridges and walkways' and the modern, electronic music of the 1960s and early 1970s.[5]

The power of *A Clockwork Orange*'s aesthetic lies in how starkly it contrasts the alienation of the post-war British city with the highly stylised attempts of the protagonist, Alex DeLarge, to break out of it through his thrill-seeking pursuit of 'ultraviolence' (dressed in a white suit, black bowler hat and false eyelashes) and his belief in the transcendent beauty of Ludwig van Beethoven's music. Kubrick is thought to have borrowed heavily from Toshio Matsumoto's film *Funeral Parade of Roses* (1969), which centres on a transgender woman in Tokyo's underground gay culture while featuring lots of sex and violence and high-speed montage scenes set to chopped-up, modern versions of classical music. (Anthony Burgess's novel *A Clockwork Orange*, published in 1962, didn't have the queer aspects, instead focussing on a government plan to condition people out of criminal behaviours through a coercive treatment, the Ludovico Technique, that induces crippling nausea whenever they are moved to violence – it is essentially a story about dehumanisation.)

To draw out the ethical complexities of depriving people of their free will even when they are consistently evil, Kubrick had to get viewers to sympathise with Alex, and Carlos's soundtrack was integral to this. The film's opening shot in the futuristic (and, seen now, quite kitsch) milk bar makes Alex and his 'droogs' look fearsomely cool; Carlos's foreboding theme enhances their enthralling sense of menace. They enter a concrete underpass at night: it's bleak and you can almost smell the piss. As they beat up a tramp just for the thrill, Carlos's Moog music plays, as it does again when they enter a writer's house and force him to watch as they rape his wife. The minimal yet expensive modern décor of the homes Alex invades contrasts markedly with the dilapidated tower block he lives in with his less-well-off parents – a lighter version of Carlos's theme plays when the architecture of Thamesmead is introduced. It turns darker as droogs Georgie and Dim rebel against Alex's leadership, leading to a fight at London's Thamesmead estate. Alex smashes them off a concrete walkway into a lake, and then slashes into them with a blade. Kubrick slows the footage and uses Carlos's score to make this quite balletic, defamiliarising the violence and directing the audience to consider it within the moral dilemma that unfolds after Georgie and Dim set up Alex to attack a woman in her home. He kills her while they wait outside; they bottle him and run away; he is arrested and his journey through the criminal justice system begins.

In the drab, definitely-not-modernist prison, Alex wears a grey suit, uses less 'Nadsat' slang (Burgess's mix of English vernacular, Russian and made-up words) and assists a priest, hoping to be released early for good behaviour. To this end, he volunteers for the Ludovico Technique: strapped to a chair with his eyes held open, he watches hours of violent footage, ranging from people being beaten up to Nazi rallies. Music plays in the cinema, and as a result he is programmed to react against his beloved Beethoven – his pleas to the officials to change the soundtrack are ignored. The treatment works and Alex, once released, is unable to defend himself when Dim and Georgie, who have joined the police, recognise and assault him. Desperate for help, he ends up at the writer's house. Once the writer

Cover of Thamesmead annual report, 1971–72, published by the GLC, showing Tavy Bridge and the Pyramid Club viewed from Binsey Walk

realises Alex led the gang who attacked him and his wife, paralysing him and causing her death, the writer tortures Alex with Beethoven's Ninth Symphony. Alex tries to kill himself by jumping out a window, only to wake up in the hospital no longer averse to sex or violence. He is visited by a government official who tells him the 'subversive' writer has been 'taken away', and that Alex will get a 'good job' in return for joining a propaganda drive to overturn negative publicity about the Ludovico Technique. He then plays Alex some Beethoven – the original arrangement, rather than Carlos's version. Alex, delighted to be able to enjoy his favourite music again, tells the audience: 'I was cured, alright.'

The place where *A Clockwork Orange* made the most impact was not Thamesmead, nor anywhere else in London. Rather, it was Sheffield, an industrial city that remained relatively prosperous throughout the 1970s, meaning that youthful rebellion became manifest more through art than politics.[6] Unlike, for instance, the Scottish post-punk band Scars, whose single 'Horrorshow' was written in Nadsat and narrated scenes from the book/film, Sheffield's The Human League were more loosely inspired by it, naming their EP *The Dignity of Labour* after a mural in the high-rise building where Alex lives. In another oblique reference, co-founders Martyn Ware and Ian Craig Marsh would next name themselves Heaven 17, after a group mentioned at the milk bar.[7] Even if Sheffield audiences had heard the Moog used by prog rock groups like Emerson, Lake & Palmer, or in Brian Eno's 'abstract blurts of synth noise' on Roxy Music's early records, Carlos's film score – still available in the UK, unlike the film – 'was simply the first time most Sheffield kids had heard full-on electronic music', hitherto limited to connoisseurs of contemporary composition.[8] (That Carlos's *Sonic Seasonings* [1972] predated Eno's 'ambient' works and likely influenced him – and post-punk musicians – has been noted.[9])

The Human League had started as The Future, a stridently avant-garde electronic act who rejected guitars and drums. Marsh used a Roland synthesiser to create percussion and textures, Ware programmed melody lines on a Korg 700S keyboard, and Adi Newton added sounds from tape recordings. They discarded their names, becoming A, B and C; shared the vocals, programming a computer to create lyrics from a set of words; and called it all the Cyclic And Random Lyric Organisation System – or CARLOS.[10] In one of the few surviving CARLOS songs, 'Blank Clocks', a few nouns, pronouns and prepositions replay in slightly different variations, musically influenced by Kraftwerk, Tangerine Dream and Wendy Carlos. But The Future soon dropped this automated writing in favour of more conventional lyrics. When record labels told them to work their compositions into 'more song-like forms', Marsh and Ware ditched Newton and found a new singer.[11]

That was Phil Oakey – a tall, androgynous man with long, lopsided hair who wore motorcycle jackets and lipstick. The group changed their name to The Human League (taken from a board game) and aimed to create genuinely popular electronic music. For live shows, they recruited Adrian Wright as 'director of visuals', turning gigs into a combination of film, photography and sound. Carlos's musical influence was most obvious on *The Dignity of Labour*, comprised of four instrumentals inspired by the Soviet space programme, with sparse percussion and arpeggiated synth sounds. The band's engagement with the dystopian world of *A Clockwork Orange*, however, was best explored in 'Blind Youth', on their debut album, *Reproduction* (1979). Here, Oakey rejected the Sex Pistols' declaration of 'no future' and struck against the idea that the urban environments created by post-war planners and architects were dystopic, saying 'high-rise living's not so bad'. Oakey's chorus mocked talk of dehumanisation, arguing for the modern city as a place where plenty of 'fun' could be had. He didn't say what sort of fun, but as he didn't see cities as necessarily depersonalising in and of themselves, he likely didn't mean the antisocial behaviour of Alex and his droogs: Oakey's view of 1970s Britain was distinctively optimistic.

Album art for The Human League's *Dignity of Labour: Pts. 1–4* (Fast Records, 1979)

The Human League's first two albums didn't quite make them the pop band of the future, not least because the production sounded old-fashioned next to Giorgio Moroder or Kraftwerk. The Undertones ridiculed them, in the song 'My Perfect Cousin', as 'art school boys', while Gary Numan took the impersonal, cold aesthetic to the top of the charts ahead of them. Marsh and Ware's ambitions to automate their performances in a '30-minute cinema you can dance to' clashed with Oakey's dreams of being a pop star. The group split: Oakey kept the name and Wright's visuals; Marsh and Ware ended up forming Heaven 17.[12] Oakey recruited a new bassist and two women vocalists who turned The Human League into a group with mass appeal, singing about love and relationships, the joys of friendship and youthful adventure. Scoring a massive hit with their album *Dare* (1981), they paved the way for many queer or androgynous electronic acts: Soft Cell, with their eyeliner and black leather jackets; Depeche Mode, with skirt-wearing songwriter Martin Gore; Eurythmics, with short-haired singer Annie Lennox; Japan, with long-haired, make-up wearing David Sylvian on vocals. Having once tried to remove all personality from their music, The Human League ended up spearheading a wave of artists who took their gender-variant self-expression from the underground into the mainstream.

The post-punk music that came out of Manchester was less optimistic – hardly surprising as its industry was dying. Disused factory buildings reminded people that the city's best days were in its Victorian past, while the post-war attempts at renovation were 'grim beyond belief', in the words of music writer Jon Savage, after he moved there in 1978.[13] That grimness could be heard in Joy Division's music, even if Ian Curtis didn't sing about architecture as directly as Oakey. It could better be seen in the BBC's *A Change of Sex* documentary, directed by David Pearson. First broadcast in 1979, Pearson follows Manchester-based Julia Grant through the gender reassignment process, showing bleak landscapes along the city's edges as she takes the train to London. The scenes where her psychiatrist at Charing Cross Hospital admonishes her for getting breast implants without his permission were as terrifying to transsexual women as the responses to Jayne County or Sandy Stone; they also recall the officials' cold indifference to Alex's suffering in *A Clockwork Orange*.

There was a direct connection between Joy Division and Wendy Carlos: band member Bernard Sumner, like Ware, was inspired by the 'fantastic ... orchestrated' synth sounds in her soundtrack to Kubrick's film.[14] Sumner built a synthesiser from a kit, adding its effects his own rhythmic guitar sounds, Stephen Morris's *motorik* drums, Peter Hook's innovative use of the bass as a lead instrument and Curtis's haunting vocals. This arrangement, greatly enhanced by Factory Records producer Martin Hannett, was widely used by British post-punk acts, especially after Curtis's death in 1980 cemented the band's legend. In this, Carlos, through *A Clockwork Orange*, did not just influence the style of 1980s pop – she also did much to shape its sound.

The theme of dehumanisation dropped out of British pop as the advent of Thatcherism brought the opposite problem: the most self-serving kind of individualism. Heaven 17 attacked this in 'Play to Win' and other tracks on *Penthouse and Pavement* (1981), but found the yuppies they criticised just identified with their ironic lyrics.[15] With electronic music now fully integrated into the mainstream, Carlos became a less direct influence. Her soundtrack to *TRON* (1982) was not cited by musicians anywhere near as frequently as her *A Clockwork Orange* soundtrack – despite *TRON*'s being far more accessible. The kind of intentional depersonalisation explored by The Future (and inspired by Kraftwerk as much as Kubrick) also became less fashionable. Likewise, the gleefully gender-variant New Romantic acts who followed The Human League declined after their mid-1980s peak.

It was another musician who fought the impulse – and imperative – to keep quiet about one's transsexual history, leading to a renaissance in trans writing, art and culture. In 1987, two years after Wendy Carlos told *People* that her transition need not have been such an issue, Sandy Stone published her essay 'The "Empire" Strikes Back: A Post-Transsexual Manifesto' on early online networks, arguing that transsexual people should talk and write more openly about their experiences as a way of breaking down prejudices from all corners of society. More than three decades later, there are still plenty of reasons to keep quiet for fear of the response, but there are now plenty of musicians, composers and listeners who were liberated by Stone's writing, and who recognise Wendy Carlos as a pioneer not just of electronic music but also trans visibility. It may not have been via the most direct route, but in both her work and her personal life, Carlos has helped several generations of people to express their humanity in their music – more than she might ever have anticipated in those dark days of the early 1970s.

Film still of Julia Grant in *A Change of Sex*, dir. David Pearson, first broadcast in 1979

1. Sarah Wooley, 'Writing "1977" for BBC Radio 4, and why it's about so much more than "a transgender woman in the 1970s"', https://www.bbc.co.uk/blogs/writersroom/entries/7c87da6e-c8b0-462e-86a9-b4227fdd25de, accessed 18 March 2021.
2. Janice G. Raymond, 'Sappho by Surgery: The Transsexually Constructed Lesbian-Feminist' (excerpted from *The Transsexual Empire: The Making of the Modern She-Male*), in *The Transgender Studies Reader* (ed. Susan Stryker and Stephen Whittle), New York: Routledge, 2006, p.135.
3. Wendy Carlos, 'On Prurient Matters', http://www.wendycarlos.com/pruri.html, accessed 18 March 2021.
4. Simon Reynolds, *Rip It Up and Start Again: Postpunk 1978–1984*, London: Faber & Faber, 2005, p.xxiv.
5. *Ibid.*
6. *Ibid.*, pp.151–52.
7. *Ibid.*
8. *Ibid.*
9. Esra Soraya Padgett, 'Where is Wendy Carlos?', *Cultured*, 2 October 2019, https://www.culturedmag.com/wendy-carlos/, accessed 10 April 2021.
10. S. Reynolds, *Rip It Up and Start Again*, op. cit., pp.160–61.
11. *Ibid.*, p.161.
12. *Ibid.*, p.322.
13. *Ibid.*, p.174.
14. *Synth Britannia*, dir. Ben Whalley (BBC, 2009).
15. *Ibid.*

Valentina
Frances Scott

VALENTINA   DIRECTIONS

                        MUSIC

                        ECHO

                        RECORDING

I'm going to press play

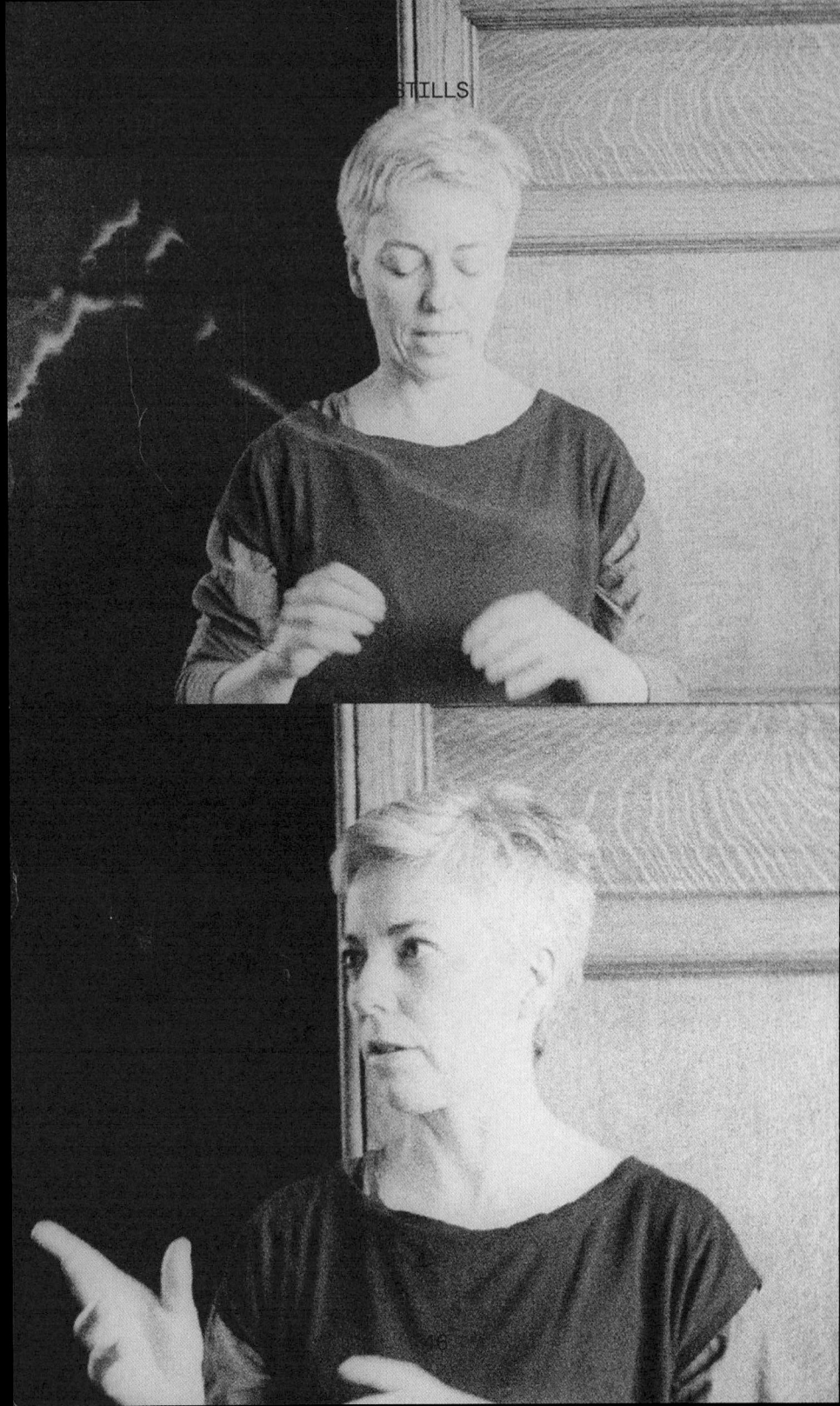

STILLS

VALENTINA	DIRECTIONS
	WOOD PANELLED ROOM WINDOW LIGHT DARKNESS VALENTINA
and, I am leaning. I'm standing, I'm leaning against a wood panel	
	CENTRE OF FRAME, WAITING
and I start moving my hands and saying 'here's Wendy the this, here's Wendy the that'	
	GESTURES, EACH A WORD
you know, 'here's Wendy the this, here's Wendy the that'	
you know, 'here's Wendy the this'	
	CLOSER
I'm saying... moving my lips, looking down, lifting my hands. Moving... and...	
	READING, LOOKING AWAY
	LOOKING BACK, LOOKING TO CAMERA
	ERROR IN THE TRANSCRIPTION PALE BLUE HIGHLIGHTER PEN 'EVERY TIME I'VE BEEN AN ECLIPSE – SHE IS THE ECLIPSE'

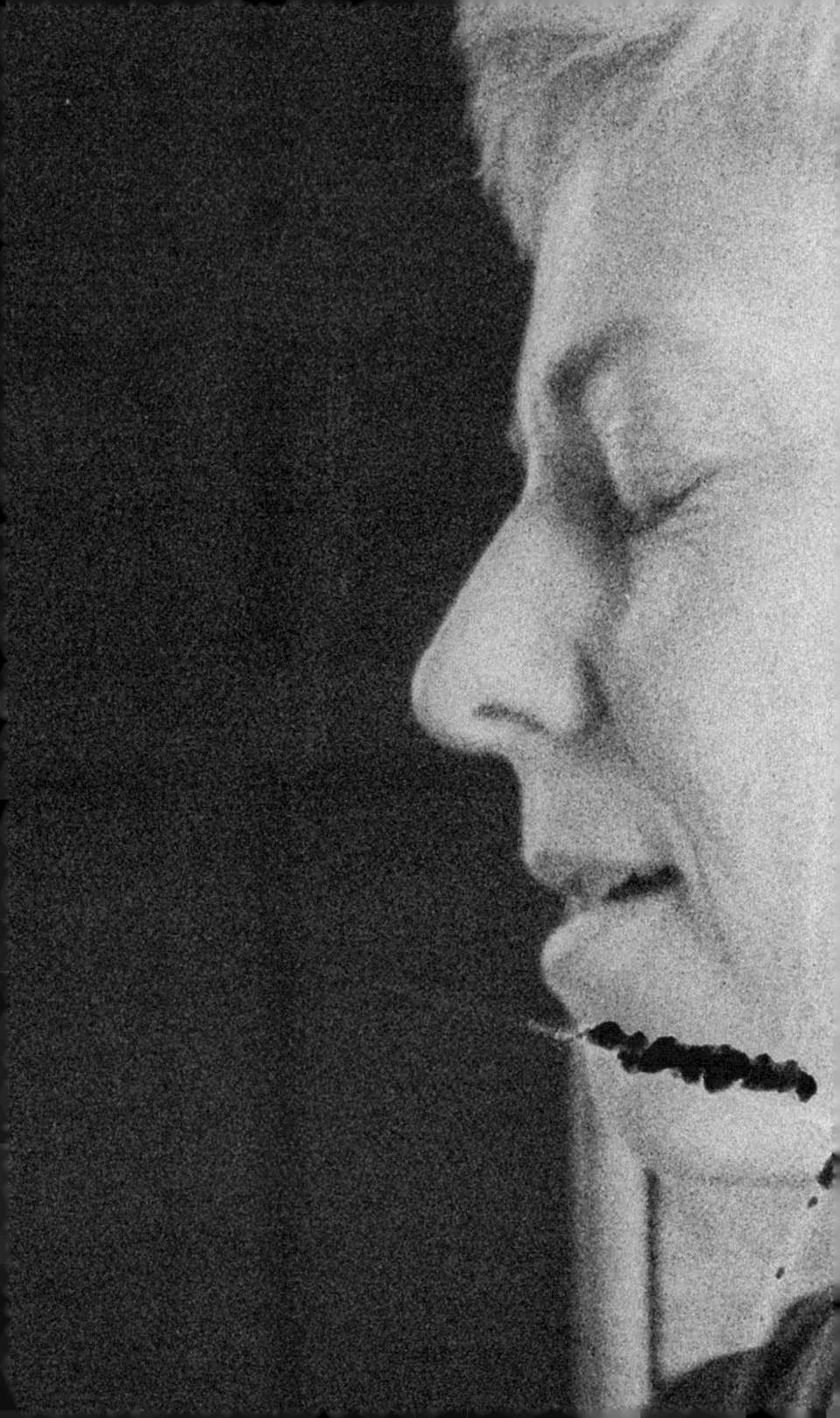

VALENTINA	DIRECTIONS

```
cartography
mapping
geography
the transformations
the math behind that
mathematics in general
physics
```

                                                CLOSER

```
cartography... not sure...
transformation
photography
the math behind that
mathematics in general
physics
```

                                       SMILING, LAUGHTER

```
acoustics, which is a
subdivision of math
astronomy
telescopes


closer

computers, both programming
and hardware
```

                                       LOOKING TO WINDOW
                                       ILLUMINATED

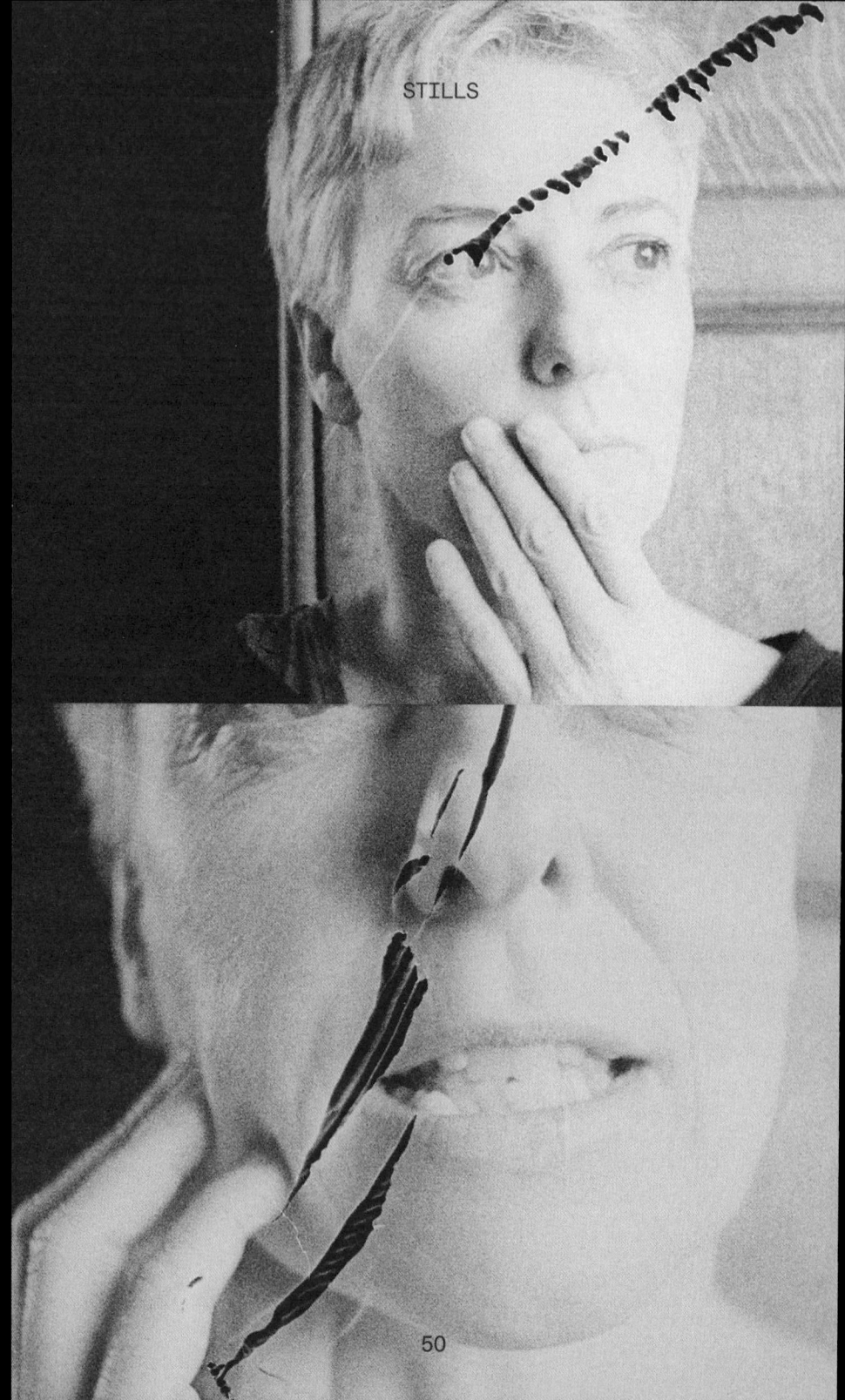

VALENTINA	DIRECTIONS
I'm looking out	
	LIPS MOVING, WORDS SILENCED
and I'm trying to remember, remembering	
in profile	
	COMING CLOSER
coming closer	
hand on my lips, I'm touching my lips	
	REVERIES = IMAGES
I mean, there are a lot of people who are Renaissance style people, I'm not the only one	
	ALMOST TOUCHING, LIPS HAND TO FACE THE CORONA OF THE SUN
	IMAGES BEFORE WORDS
the corona of the sun, the corona of the sun, the corona of the sun,	

STILLS

VALENTINA   DIRECTIONS

moving left to right, across,
left to right

                              BODY DRIFT

left to right

STILLS

VALENTINA   DIRECTIONS

55

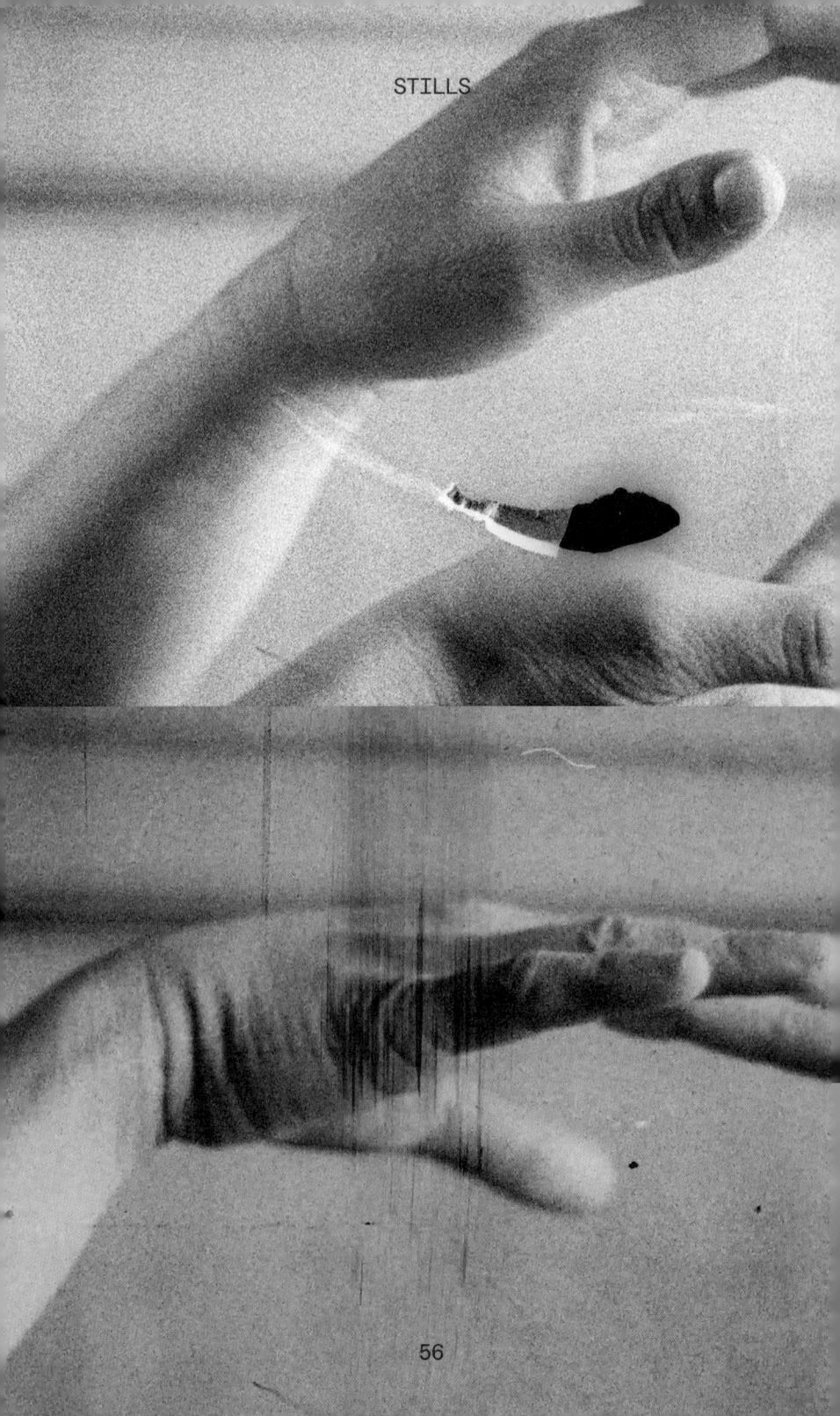
STILLS

VALENTINA	DIRECTIONS
	FINGERTIPS, OBSCURING

<table>
<tr><td>lifting my hands, my hands
are going side to side,
shifting from one side to
the other</td><td></td></tr>
<tr><td>you know, like, one hand up,
one hand down</td><td></td></tr>
<tr><td>you know,
'here's Wendy the this,
here's Wendy the that'</td><td></td></tr>
<tr><td></td><td>HANDS, CUPPING</td></tr>
<tr><td>switching, like an eclipse
making a circle
shaping, my hands, shaping</td><td></td></tr>
<tr><td></td><td>FORM UNSEEN
BURST OF LIGHT</td></tr>
<tr><td>making an eclipse
and down
shaping an eclipse.</td><td></td></tr>
<tr><td></td><td>MUSIC</td></tr>
<tr><td></td><td>TITLES</td></tr>
<tr><td></td><td>PULSES</td></tr>
</table>

Valentina
a film by Frances Scott

Camera, edit
Frances Scott

Sound design, vocoder
Chu-Li Shewring

Music
Tom Richards on Mini Oramics

Valentina
Valentina Formenti

Transcription
Will Brady

Film processing
Bea Haut

Telecine
Steve Oakes, Images4Life

Titles
An Endless Supply

Thanks
Phil Coy, Valentina Formenti, Mat Jenner, Music Division – New York Public Library, Ragnhild Olsen and Greenwich Dance Agency, Tom Richards, Chu-Li Shewring and Dave Tompkins

Filmed in the Long Gallery at Charlton House, South London, February 2020.

Wendy, eclipsing

Stine Hebert

Wendy Carlos witnessed her first solar eclipse in the summer of 1963 in Dexter, Maine in the United States — the event lasted less than two minutes, of which she witnessed '62 memorable seconds'.[1] The maximum duration of a total solar eclipse is 7 minutes and 32 seconds, no matter where on Earth the phenomenon is experienced. After her initial encounter in Maine, Carlos travelled to different destinations around the world to view and capture solar eclipses. Total solar eclipses can be seen approximately every eighteen months somewhere on Earth and are only possible to observe indirectly – they will cause permanent damage to the retina unless mediated by specialist equipment. Carlos's pursuit of these brief, rare celestial events, and the innovative photographic methods she prototyped to image them, have been highly influential in an ever-developing field, appearing in magazines such as *Astronomy* and *Sky & Telescope* and used by the US government's National Aeronautics and Space Administration (more commonly known as NASA).[2]

Solar eclipses occur on what is called the 'new moon': when the moon travels in the passage between the sun and Earth, it momentarily casts a shadow that blocks the sun from being seen on Earth. Thus, for a short while a solar eclipse can profoundly alter your perception of your immediate surroundings.

Carlos herself has taken a step back from appearing publicly. Today her website is the most direct source of her thinking; ultimately, as the main interface to contextualise her practice, it gives voice to her music, her composition work and her cosmological interests. On this platform, Carlos reveals her fascination for solar eclipses:

> You will witness the day become near-night, like the deepest twilight. Sunset colors bathe the full horizon, while a gaping black hole gazes down at you from the inky sky, eye-like and surreal, surrounded by the solar corona, a halo of pearly ephemeral light of delicate beauty. Each time the corona looks quite different, and like an old friend's face you'll recognize each in photographs.[3]

CAPTURING AN EVENT

Wendy Carlos constitutes the focal point of Frances Scott's new film *Wendy*, a work still in the making at the time of writing. This is perhaps telling of the entire process of the project, which Scott herself describes as a 'fan letter': a first-person address that signals familiarity, or distance with intimate knowledge. And yet, *Wendy* isn't a portrait of Wendy Carlos. Carlos is an elusive figure who has deliberately withdrawn from public life. She has restricted access to herself, giving few interviews and making limited public appearances; and still the interest in her and her work remains vast. These facts are important, as they have undoubtably influenced Scott's approach to the project, motivating her to be drawn to certain material and informing the choices she has made about how ideas are articulated and presented.

Scott's journey towards making this film, as with her other moving-image works, is heavily research-oriented but distinct from films employing a more formal, documentary methodology. The objective is not to uncover untold facts and facets of a subject or protagonist; rather, the intent is to respect and acknowledge the source material as it is revealed, and to let an associative approach determine how information is conveyed. The viewers are left to make their own connections from the assemblage: the work is primarily driven by non-linear narratives that avoid providing clear guidance as to their reading, leaving room for a distinctly responsive visual style. Rather than approaching this filmic fan letter through a predetermined process – as an uncritical homage – the course of the project's production is defined by a constant circling that leaves things in perpetual motion. Not to be confused with uncertainty due to the lack of fixture, this allows for an intimate sensibility and a highly personal reading of the material, where Scott's camera functions as a witness – a process that connects with Carlos's witnessing of the eclipse and the photographic mediation of the event.

The music score and weave of sounds for the film-in-progress, developed with Scott's collaborators Chu-Li Shewring and Tom Richards, gently guide the encounter with the work, and assist in connecting her visual and archival research with the various voices at play in the devoted search for Wendy. The somewhat unconventional order of the project – making a book about the making of the film before the film has been made, and thereby allowing the reader of the book to precede the viewer of the film – is a process that shares a resemblance with Carlos's legendary soundtrack for Stanley Kubrick's film *A Clockwork Orange* (1971). Carlos began her original composition 'Timesteps' in response to reading Anthony Burgess's novel, published almost a decade prior to the film adaptation. In other words, she began the process of writing the music, unaware of plans for the film's production. Her work relates directly to the literature and the potential of the film, but did not follow from the immediate coupling of image and sound that might be more commonly associated with scoring for cinema. Scott's approach in some ways mirrors this process, because it also entails the separation of

Marion Bradshaw's photograph of a total solar eclipse in Maine, US, 20 July 1963 – Wendy Carlos's 'first totality'

image and sound. This separation can be further imagined in footage taken of the film conservation process in which the gelatin layer – the image layer – is shown being removed from a degrading cellulose nitrate substrate: the peeling away of synthesised strata to reveal its distinct elements and composition.

VALENTINA, MOVING

A primary source of inspiration for the making of *Wendy* was Scott's encounter with the material omitted from Wendy Carlos's 1979 interview with Arthur Bell for *Playboy* magazine. Through this interview, Carlos became one of the first figures to speak publicly about not identifying with the gender assigned to her at birth and about transitioning. The *Playboy* interview was heavily edited from the original sound recordings, and crucial elements of Carlos and Bell's conversations do not appear in the published text. Scott located audio files of two of the cassette tapes from the interview sessions, now held in the Rodgers and Hammerstein Archives of Recorded Sound in the Music Division of the New York Public Library. After transcribing these tapes, it became apparent that Bell's preferred focus (or that of his editors) had been on the details of Carlos's transition, which, considering the context of *Playboy* magazine, isn't too surprising. Carlos invested many hours in multiple meetings with Bell and was most likely disappointed by the outcome, which does not feature a holistic presentation of her practice, and her cosmic interests are all but erased.[4] The published *Playboy* exchange remains one of Carlos's few public interviews; thereafter she agreed in the main to speak only with journalists for publications that showed an interest in focussing on her music. Scott holds a particular interest in the excluded material from the conversations between Carlos and Bell, and her work *Valentina* (2020), which is a prelude to *Wendy*, is an attempt to give voice and body to the value of Carlos's articulation of her passions and professional achievements in 1979 that only partially made their way to the public.

The protagonist in *Valentina* – who is in fact the performer and dancer Valentina Formenti – responds through movement to Scott's transcripts of the tapes exploring Carlos's interests and proficiency in photography, astronomy, mathematics and more. Valentina, in *Valentina*, presents an unearthly double presence. She speaks indirectly, her words recalling Carlos's responses to Bell's questions. Through this process of remembering, she physically manifests and brings to life the ideas discussed in the interview. Her voice isn't directly synced with the footage, as the initial filming was made as part of a series of tests during a performance rehearsal using a 16mm camera (a Bolex H16, Scott's usual choice) that does not capture sound. The voice-over was captured after the filming via an online video call during the Covid-19 pandemic 'lockdown' in Spring 2020. The sound recording was later processed through a vocoder to transform the voice by coding it into control signals and then decoding them back into audible speech – adding another layer that does not fully conform to our expectations of synchronicity.

For the viewer, the question of which ideas and visual representations come to the fore and which recede is diffuse and unpredictable. At one point, Valentina performs the shape of an eclipse – the circle of the corona of the sun – with her hands, which gestures to how the distortion and shadowing occurring in the work is elusive and impossible to fully identify.

Carlos's fascination with the phenomenon of the solar eclipse seems to have strongly resonated with Scott and her mode of production. Scott's methodological approach to the material could be read as a reverse eclipse of the person in focus, revealing certain information and concealing, or drawing into shadow, other details. In this way, she allows previously underappreciated aspects of her subject to fill up the arena while simultaneously studying the qualities that make up a film – a recurrent theme in Scott's practice. By enabling temporary exposure to the excluded material, which may in fact be the most crucial and personal information available, *Valentina*, and next *Wendy*, open up spaces for these ideas to come back to life as new presences and perceptions of Carlos's oeuvre.

LISTENING TO THE MAGICAL VOYAGES

Remarkably, the very first moving-image footage made of a solar eclipse was captured in 1900 by the magician Nevil Maskelyne, in the US state of North Carolina. Maskelyne was a professional illusionist and profoundly invested in blurring the lines between magic and science. His film is an example of early cinema and science brought together within a magical context. The capturing of the solar eclipse – the sun momentarily hidden from view – appears in Maskelyne's film as the greatest magic trick ever. If the eclipse brings with it questions of visibility, and dynamics of power and control, it ultimately, if only temporarily, disrupts the normative hierarchy of information.

Theorist, curator and writer Paul B. Preciado's most recent book, *An Apartment on Uranus: Chronicles of the Crossing* (2020), collects essays he wrote between 2013–18. Preciado poetically unfolds the circumstances involved in what he describes as his processes of transitioning, including the societal reactions, and his personal reflections on the experience. The undoing of notions of gender and the technological circumstances and biopolitical conditions involved in enabling such processes greatly affect not just the production and reception of a body, but the understanding of the voice stemming from it.

Preciado details the complications of having a voice in transitioning. He states:

> But what does it mean to speak for those who have been refused access to reason and knowledge, for us who have been regarded as mentally ill? With what voice can we speak? [...] To speak is to invent the language of the crossing, to project one's voice into an interstellar expedition: to translate our difference into the language of the norm; while we continue, in secret, to practice a strange lingo that the law does not understand.[5]

When Carlos spoke to Arthur Bell in 1979, the world perhaps looked very different than it does today. Yet in the *Playboy* interview Carlos remarks that the great fear associated with revealing her transition had been a much heavier burden to carry than any potential stigma.[6] Preciado also writes of his experience:

> I am a dissident of the sex-gender system. I am the multiplicity of the cosmos trapped in a binary political and epistemological system, shouting in front of you. I am a Uranian confined inside the limits of techno-scientific capitalism. [...] I am bringing no news from the margins; instead, I bring you a piece of horizon.[7]

This 'horizon' might share some of the same skyline that Scott alludes to in *Wendy*. In her approach to gathering and drawing from little-known or unheard/unseen material, Scott returns our attention to Wendy Carlos within the frame of her life's work, as a public persona who actively resists aspects of her publicness. Scott is invested in deliberately raising the question of what may be shadowing the readings of potential identities? What manifests itself to the eye, and what withdraws from view? *Wendy* is a speculative portrait, and this portrait is constantly evolving, continuously contributing to the making of the final film, a never-ending possibility. Perhaps, in this sense, it is also temporarily eclipsing, by gently veiling what is otherwise too bright to be perceived.

Film frames from Nevile Maskelyne's footage of a solar eclipse in North Carolina, US, 28 May 1900

The artist and writer Salomé Voeglin, who specialises in sonic explorations and the phenomenology of auditory cultures, raises this important question: What does it mean to listen to someone on their own terms? People who are not in charge of their own representation, who may exist in socially marginalised positions, are rendered vulnerable. The intention of directing attention to such positions of under- or misrepresentation involves challenging aspects of an ethics of listening. Voeglin says: 'To listen is an openness [...] to be ready to receive whatever kind of response that may form.'[8] This also means tuning in to something one doesn't recognise, and receiving without knowing the mode of transmission in advance.

With *Wendy*, Scott has made the choice to hold Wendy Carlos in constant orbit around her. She is unable and unwilling to pin her down, and instead invested in opening up an understanding of those elements that might be underrepresented or eclipsed. Scott's research brings to light what has been held in the archive; her filmmaking provides a new lens to those nuances and complexities otherwise missing from previously visible narratives. *Wendy* is not a film about Wendy Carlos, but a film about her interests and wide-reaching practice. In this way, it is a political contribution to the reading of Carlos's oeuvre and work.

1   Wendy Carlos, 'Total Solar Eclipse Page', http://www.wendycarlos.com/eclipse.html, accessed 3 May 2021.
2   William Stephenson, 'The well-tempered synthesizer: Wendy Carlos's music of the spheres', *Harper's Magazine*, October 2020, p.88.
3   W. Carlos, 'Total Solar Eclipse Page', http://www.wendycarlos.com/eclipse.html, accessed 3 May 2021.
4   W. Carlos interviewed by Arthur Bell, *Playboy*, May 1979, p.76.
5   Paul B. Preciado, *An Apartment on Uranus: Chronicles of the Crossing* (trans. Charlotte Mandell), London: Fitzcarraldo, 2020, ebook p.26.
6   W. Carlos interviewed by A. Bell, *op. cit.*, p.81.
7   P.B. Preciado, *An Apartment on Uranus, op. cit.*, ebook p.29.
8   Salomé Voegelin, 'Care-full Listening', Rupert online talk, 10 December 2020, https://rupert.lt/online-talk-care-full-listening/, accessed 5 May 2021.

Their waving signals a moon

Dave Tompkins

Orbited by Wendy Carlos

I. MIDNIGHT, THE STARS AND MOOG

Annie Coulter tells her father she's attending a midnight screening of *Fantasia*. He's a high-level vocoder consultant for the US State Department, working in voice security. She's a teenage pacifist using Disney as a cover to see *A Clockwork Orange*.

Beethoven, hair rewired, bleeds through theatre walls in northern Virginia. A mouse in a megaphone hat drifts off, ears dished under a conical night sky. Wooden brooms march to a vocode to joy, while a goon in a bowler gets punted into a lake. Big night at the Tyson's Corner Cinema in 1971. It replays in Annie's head during the ride home, filtered through the soundtrack by Wendy Carlos, the Moog overdubbed and looped into scenes by memory's version. Interiors amplified. The future appeared bleak, violent and fascist, but Annie, who would become a costume designer, returned to its dystopic projection. The film's holographic glitter walls and orange tulip chairs became design cachet, while the police state remains ever present. And there would be Wendy Carlos, modulating the settings, altering the visualisation of sound.

Annie gets home from not seeing *Fantasia* as her father, Dave Coulter, emerges from his vocoder lab in the basement.[1] He'd spent the evening walled in by twinkling Pentagon computers, stretching phonemes and quarantining unvoiced sounds from voiced. Nasal murmurs gathered in his headphones, then his head.

Annie remembers her dad often 'speaking in Martian', due to their generational abyss as much as the unearthly caterwaul heard through the kitchen floor vents, discarnate frequencies of speech

Annie Coulter in her family home at Christmas, 1969

trying to find their way into Richard Nixon's snooping ear or Henry Kissinger's war crime backchannelling.² While Dave Coulter's work in crypto-telecom helped enable policies in Vietnam and Cambodia that his daughter opposed (she knew how to shut down a dinner), they bonded in the Moog patches of Wendy Carlos. Annie was prohibited from her father's 'batman computer cave' and from listening to the soundtrack of *A Clockwork Orange* up in her room, but they found common ground in the living room, where *Switched-On Bach* became a household standard. An aspiring pianist, her father often played Beethoven and Bach. 'Air on a G String' on piano, then Carlos's synth version on the record player. Annie's mother, Freddie Coulter (a psychologist whom a twelve-year-old Annie took to see Bob Marley), joined in on harpsichord.

Baroque synths reconfigure the Coulters' sunken living room, tone-colouring the hardwood floors and glass walls.

Furniture oscillates. The rosewood cadenza, the Windsor chairs, the octangular coffee table. Plug the sectional over there, a derangement of modular set pieces, next to the laughing teenager in striped, green bell-bottoms.³

```
The vocoder
was a proto-
type we worked
on together. It
was experimental,
a little crude and
far less costly
than several
later commercial
'luxury'
vocoders.
```

~~~~~~~~~~~~~~~~~

Wendy Carlos first met Bob Moog at an AES convention in 1964, a year after she photographed her first eclipse. Perks of AES membership included sneak previews of a vocoder demonstration at the New York World's Fair that year. For a starstruck Moog, it would lead him to Dave Coulter: he'd been seeking out the vocoder engineer ever since reading about his research in tunable formants, imagining how to conform the acoustic energy of phonetics to his synthesisers. At an AES lecture in 1974, Annie watched them nerd out over the future: a through-wave from the Pentagon vocoder in her dad's man-machine cave to Moog's modular walls and, ultimately, to Wendy, an umbraphile who saw the 'anarchy of total possibility' in electronic music.⁴

```
Audio
Engineering
Society Convention
(AES): I said
'Alright, where's
the vocoder?!' They
said, 'Oh, you're right
beside it.' And there
was a large beige moulded
fibreglass cabinet that
reached up to my chin,
with sloping streamlined
sides. You only saw a
couple of switches and a
power light that was on.
It was quiet. I pressed
my ear against it,
but could hear no
fans. Of course.
Solid State!
```

Moog had read about Coulter's formants in a restricted report published in 1962 by Melpar, a defence and aerospace contractor that offered electronic battle simulation as well as vocoders for government phones and satellite systems. At the time, another of Coulter's employers, the US Naval Research Laboratory, was using the vocoder to communicate with a pair of dolphins named Dash and Dopey. The Navy's Man-to-Dolphin Translator (MDT) improved upon their Man-to-Porpoise Integrated communication system (MPI), converting modulated whistles into 'humanoid vocal sounds'. *Bip burrap yump.*[5]

While the dolphins laughed at the Navy's efforts at cetacean recruitment,[6] the vocoder went to sea, serving a triangulation of aircraft carriers stationed in the Gulf of Tonkin. Coulter's Metavox partner Frank Gentges monitored voice security in the hull of the *USS Bon Homme*, beneath the mess hall which doubled as bomb storage. Codenamed MF STEAMVALVE,[7] the system digitised orders regarding air strikes and human targets in Vietnam, a binary reduction. 1 for voiced, 0 for unvoiced. Airwaves versus ground.

On the vocoder's struggles with clarity, Gentges shared in an interview, 'The relationship to reality was not very good.'[8] As if the machine was attuned to US policy, on dissonant terms with reality as well.

> They had a visual display with a pitch follower so you could sing into it. It could detect the pitch and little bulbs would light up on a musical scale to show you what pitch you were hearing. They'd harness someone from the audience to come up and talk and sing as well. And I got nailed to do that. They would raise the pitch to a squeaky sound or down to a Darth Vader effect, and ask, 'Why are you here?' Like a dopey television quiz programme — nothing that needed to be saved for posterity. But I found it whimsical and affectionate. I set aside in my mind that someday, some way, I wanted a vocoder!

> Not that the vocoder and synthetic speech were state secrets. Now they're almost clichés. But they certainly were cutting-edge and highly unusual at the time.

II. RESONATOR MEMBRANE

A B-52 Stratofortress flies over Tây Lộc, Central Vietnam. Clouds hum to the mountains west. Below, tubular droning on farmland. The Tà Ôi, an indigenous group of animist highlanders, modulate their voices with *A'bel*, a bamboo instrument deployed in the ancient practice of sharing vibrations. Courtship resonates through opposite ends of the tube, throats shaping the harmonics. It's a Talk Box duet: computer love channelled from reeds in pond craters. The *A'bel* bamboo tone-mapped the landscape long before bombs deforested the topography, deployed by abstracted orders from higher-ups, voices removed.

~~~~~~~~~~~~~~~~~~~~~~~~~~~~~

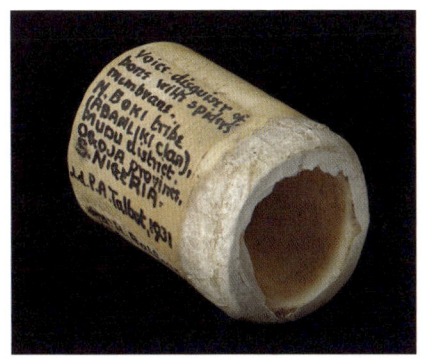

Laryngeal cartography, the mapping of speech resonances, can sonify the deceased, from Goethe's voice box to the Egyptian priest Nasyamun ('True of Voice'), whose final wish was to continue speaking and catching sunsets after death. Working with 3D models in 2020, researchers in Leeds used an electrolarynx to reconstruct Nasyamun's vocal tract three thousand years after he was felled by an insect and an allergic reaction. The mummy speaks! But what of? The spider that silenced him? At the Symposium of Pharocoders, a keynote speaker wrapped in recording tape (Egyptian Lover master reels, if one must) discussed the arachnoid origins of West African voice disguisers. The Boki, pioneers in biotremology, have used bees wax to glue spider silk inside a ram's femur, creating a membranous resonator.[9] Spirits and ancestors intonated through retuned spider threads.

May they summon the late Roger Troutman of Zapp, who was once carried to the stage like an Ohio funk pharaoh in LED underwear. Roger's posthumous single with South Kak, 'Freaky Dreams', is a Talk Box tube from the subconscious, left unfinished in the studio, melody contoured from the raw infrastructure of his resonances. Auto-Tune is a séance for Roger, even if the medium is a cheap smartphone apparition. Released in 2001, two years after his death, 'Freaky Dreams' played three times in a row when it debuted on an Atlanta radio station. The dream recurrent, blinking awake.[10]

Voice disguiser (c.1925) made by the Boki peoples of South Nigeria and constructed from the leg bone of a ram, open at one end (the mouthpiece) and closed with spider's membrane at the other

Roger Troutman of Zapp, promotional photograph, 1980

III. THE SEMBLANCE OF THE THING BENEATH

At a mental health facility in Bavaria, psychiatrists played vocoder recordings for patients while they slept, hoping 'talking water drops' could seep into their dreams. In New York, neuroscientists at Columbia University programmed vocoder algorithms to interpret brain pulses, translating thoughts into speech. Stroke victims and patients with speech afflictions could then communicate with Alexa, in a sort of telepathic vocoder-to-vocoder sound system. If neural patterns can train the vocoder, could the vocoder then read our minds back to us?

Ute Holl, a professor of media studies at the University of Basel, once told me the vocoder could be technology as framework for memory,[11] keeping in mind that it was originally intended for bandwidth contraction over phone lines. In 1945, the US government's Office of Scientific Research and Development imagined that Bell Labs' text-to-speech keyboard, the Voder, would serve as part of a 'memory extending desk'.[12] Vocoders and memories operate through filtre banks, channels, distortions, degradations and disbanded frequencies, conversations between the past and technology. Some memories are processed through the voice of another. A parent, a sibling, a lover. A surrogate whisper. What we've been told mingles with our own patchy reconstructions. A fragment from 'Love's Old Sweet Song', versioned through a Bell Labs vocoder demo in the 1930s, returns as a letter to the past itself: *Dear dead days beyond recall.*

~~~~~~~~~~~~~~~~~~~~~~~~~~~~~~

Lieutenant Dorothy L. Madsen, ninety-seven and racing to finish a memoir before losing her sight, remembers the vocoder through tubes of light. Tiny glass vacuums of space and random heat converted to encryption. From 1944 to 1946, Madsen oversaw operations at the Global Encrypted Conference Center at the Pentagon, acting as a vocoder interpreter while sitting in on calls between generals and heads of state. A crucial link, she distilled speech from the vocoder's flawed 'frequency discriminator' for men uncomfortable

Bell System's Voder float at Golden Gate Exposition, San Francisco, 1940

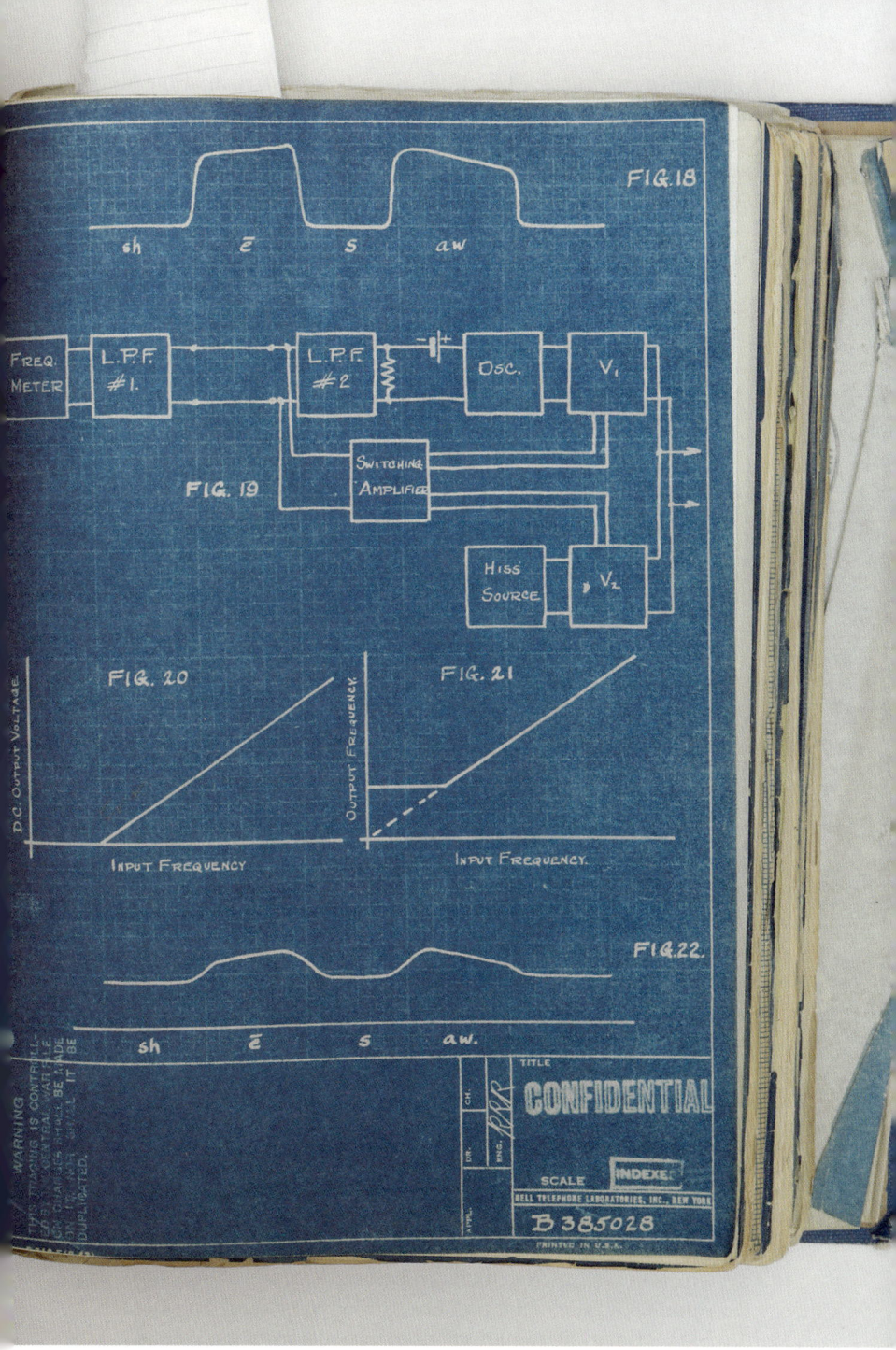

Bell Labs' classified 'secrecy system' vocoder bible (vol. 1, 1932–45). 'She Saw' input frequency diagram

with their own robotness. This could mean fielding a rush order for tank antennae to Normandy or an incoming call from Joseph Stalin, who ordered a Gulag to build a vocoder to protect his phone from the paranoid feedback loop inside his head. In early May 1945, just before V-E Day, Madsen prompted Harry Truman on her legal pad, descrambling Adolf Hitler's cerebral hemorrhage during the president's conversation with Winston Churchill.

Several floors below, occupying (and overheating) 2500 square feet in the Pentagon basement, the machine tasked with voice compression became the space itself, all the while maintaining a fake address on an upper floor. Signal Corps officers claimed the system codename SIGSALY just stood for nonsense. Yet it recalls a child hustling conchs by the sea, waves from white noise, shore to shush. Engineers referred to it as an approximation of speech, a spectral description. For Madsen, frequency bands of compression come to mind as frequency bands of light.

Leslie Groves, director of the Manhattan Project, attempted to access SIGSALY with a bogus grocery list. Madsen blocked him. 'He made up this code of his own, which consisted of groceries', she later remembered. 'So when he came to the conference center, he'd start peeling off these groceries. That's when my staff said, "He can't use this system, he's just talking about groceries."'[13]

'You didn't pay much attention to what was being said', said Donald Mehl, a Signal Corps lieutenant monitoring calls from the Pentagon

Lt. Dorothy Madsen (right) with Lt. R. Burckhardt (left), c.1942

basement. 'You focused on the transmission.'[14] Mehl kept hearing the words 'Manhattan Project' but knew nothing of its meaning, only that the voice be understood. Though SIGSALY transcriptions were destroyed, a phrase concerning the Manhattan Project survives in fragments of oral histories from the archives of the National Security Agency (NSA): 'Hell-bomb'. The spectral description names the unspeakable, illuminating what cannot be imagined.

~~~~~~~~~~~~~~~~~~~~~~~~~~~

The vocoder's plight to put words together may have given Madsen a phonetic ear. 'When I get into that memory bank, the more things come to light.' She held onto the wine glasses she used as bug detectors. After returning home from a triple shift, cleared for a drink, she'd wet her finger and circle the rim of her Waterford crystal glass, listening for feedback. The crystal chime signals memory pitched in higher frequency. According to Bell Labs, the vocoder often failed to recognise women's voices. 'Pitch bias', a common term in amp schemata, by design.[15]

In the early 1970s, when Madsen was still prohibited from speaking of SIGSALY, electronic composer Suzanne Ciani collaborated with German synth engineer Harald Bode on a vocoder filter that acknowledged the airier parts of her speech. 'I needed a modification. Something less metallic and masculine. Because you're not hearing the breathy part of the voice [in the vocoder], which is usually happening in a very high feminine range. We built a pass-through so my breath could come through with the sound. The vocoder was for adding warmth – a melodic sustained wash of a vocal presence. It was sensual. It had this beauty of being somewhere between an instrument and a human presence.'[16] Ciani's work in television and film flourished in this ambiguity (once disrupting David Letterman in the process[17]), opening up and subverting channels previously restricted to military brass who feared sounding like Donald Duck.[18]

IV. *AHEM!*

July 2020. A synth dirge that once lured us into a traumatised resort, off-season, returns to deter tourists from Disney World. Someone has edited Wendy Carlos and Rachel Elkind's main theme for *The Shining* into an ad announcing the 'grandemic' reopening of the Magic Kingdom. Masking complies with overdubs as employees warn 'it's not safe', revealing Disney to be asynchronous with the times. Carlos's funeral march brought things up to speed. A clean sheet levitates over a hotel bed, rippling in slow motion to Elkind's banshee trill. A vacuum glides across an empty room. The *TRON* Lightcycle ride, from the Disney film scored by Carlos in 1982, remains in the dark.[19]

~~~~~~~~~~~~~~~~~~~~~~~~~~~~~~

Pandemic voices are masked, aerosolic threats. When Florian Schneider passed away in April 2020, a friend in Munich sent a file: Kraftwerk opening a live performance with Carlos's score for the Ludovico Technique in *A Clockwork Orange*. He said the first time he saw Kraftwerk he returned from Mars on a stretcher. 'Let's compute', my friend wrote, his default code for meeting in person. The algorithm sensed distancing, by road trip. A Volkswagen ad appeared on my screen, tone-deaf but tuned-in. An office worker, crossing a skyway in some generic now-future. He is 'Mister Blue Sky', a top-down yearner caught in an ELO daydream. He pauses to moon over a red convertible, imagining himself driving a car whose engine once spoke ('I'm dyyyiiinng') through a vocoder developed by Munich-based Siemens. Florian first heard the Siemens demo tape in the '60s. The rest is Autobahn.[20]

```
You
meet the
strangest
people these
days when you
happen to be
carrying a
vocoder around
with you.
Ever notice
that?
```

I once tried to interest Florian in a dragon from Venus. The dragon had six eyes and wore a phonetic keyboard strapped to its chest, using its tendrils to intonate in Cockney. The speech keyboard was a portable version of the Voder, a Bell Labs invention that astonished crowds at the 1939 New York World's Fair, mastered by telephone operators called Voderettes. In Robert Heinlein's *Between Planets* (1951), the dragon plays the Voder for throat clearance, descrambling a frog in the key of phlegm. *EH-HEM!* It could also be announcing a presence: the unseen switchboard operators who trained for a year to enable the Voder to speak in the first place.

I asked Doug Slocum, a synth designer who recreated the Voder, about what combination of keys and pedals could manufacture said noise. 'I haven't seen a setting on the original that could do a gargling type sound as you describe. They probably didn't think of it, though without such sounds, many languages would not have been possible to produce.' This vibration, deep in the Grover, can signal a 'boundary artefact' of speech, both a reminder of shared space and the constrictions of English.

Original cover illustration by Darrell K. Sweet for Robert A. Heinlein's *Between Planets* (Ballantine Books, 1978) featuring a 'dragon from Venus' wearing a phonetic keyboard

Florian's reply to my dragon query was its own *ahem*. *If U R going to believe all this Fantasy stuff, U will never come 2 an end.* Wendy Carlos would agree, once writing that, like her, I'd never be free of the vocoder.

During the pandemic, I revisit old notes, some vocoder-related, some remotely related. One file, labelled 'No UFOs', concerns a series of cease-and-desist robocalls received in 1968 by the assistant editor of *Saucer News*, Jack Robinson. 'An electronic-type voice, definitely not human, told me to stop all saucer research. It sounded like the strange kind of "voice" that might be produced by a Voder machine. Each time, the message has been the same: "Stop all saucer research."'[21]

A week after Florian's passing, I take a scroll through the online archives of the Smithsonian Speech Synthesis History Project. I'm looking for Kurtis Blow, impersonated by the Votrax, a phonemic text-to-speech synth developed by the Federal Screw Works, an automotive parts supplier in Detroit. The going is blurry. There are tongue-twisters in Japanese, police response systems, and reports from the Pillsbury Data Center. If you're looking for disconnection, the voice in service of a dead phone line is here.

But no Kurtis Blow. Florian's Votrax pursuits included playing parts of Blow's 1982 rap 'The Boogie Blues' by hand. The phoneme transcripts are classified, somewhere between Detroit and Düsseldorf, but the phonemes themselves remain with Kurtis, held close in the memories of kids who knew all the words.

Recent studies have found that speech-recognition tech used by Google, Facebook and Amazon expose a 'racial divide' in transcribing, or just hearing, Black voices. Again by design, as it's mainly white programmers who control the vocal biometrics.[22] Jay-Z doesn't remember reading the Book of Genesis through a vocoder, but Tacotron 2 does. Google's text-to-speech AI holds Jay's false memory in phonemes and digital spectrograms, using a vocoder to synthesise time-domain waveforms from his voice. It makes for a convincing deepfake, so real that Jay-Z sued for his own properties of speech.[23]

Is speech compression a flattening? The vocoder hasn't been the most inclusive of machines – once described as a 'representation of voice', yet intended to reduce. Deemed an unintelligible failure for public telephone discourse, and redacted from the lips of its users during the war, this device intended to improve telecommunications was kept in the hands and throats of a white power minority. Through hip-hop, R&B and disco, the vocoder would open up new party lines, bringing much freak joy to the dancefloor, across race and gender. (And crisscrossed by queer electro artists Man Parrish and Patrick Cowley.) Disembodying the voice while bringing bodies together, whatever the robotness might've lacked in 'warmth' was compensated for in feeling, sweat and Verycheri's '69 Cancer Sign' of 1983. Florian often referred to the voice as 'artificial', but what is more real, or more human, than wanting to be something else altogether? Or all together? The vocoder could multiplex voices from one, creating multitudes of self. This could also be the delusion of listening to your own chorus.

_{The reality was simple and rather elegant.}

Laurie Anderson, who in 1981 interrogated the petrochem military in 'O Superman', once told me the vocoder could be a medium to step outside of yourself. 'I want to feel empathy and be able to go to another person's position.'[24] As the R&B producer Teddy Riley would say, 'You have to get uncomfortable when using the vocoder. Really uncomfortable.'[25]

V. BACK TO YOU

Annie Coulter's memory of her father plays back from an Xmas vocoder at the 1964 World's Fair. His Santa Claus baritone, pitched in various speeds, then *ho-ho-ho* reversed. Kids liked the exhibit so much they broke it. Annie also recalls EVA II, another Dave Coulter invention that dazzled at the fair. An experimental chart reader, the Electrical Voice Analog II interpreted spectrograms into speech, using visible formant patterns printed onto Mylar. The ink was conductive. Purchased by the NSA and later discarded, EVA II languished in a scrapyard in Upper Marlboro, Maryland until Coulter and Frank Gentges chanced upon it during a junk dive in 1974, reunited with the synth that once said, 'Neat plans fail without luck.'

Gentges was mystified by the stash of satellite photos he found among the voice prints. As if EVA II had self-upgraded from spectrograms to space, reading the stars to a junkyard on clear nights, voice metallic and shining, reflecting zodiac signs off disembodied doors, cosmic carburetors and distortions of scrap. The satellites themselves had been bouncing compressed speech signals back to Earth, through a series of intelligibility tests that Gentges called a 'vocoder confusion matrix'. What does *sub chuck gust* sound like on its return from the space? Mars on a stretcher?[26]

Gentges wore seven ballpoint pens in his shirt pocket and drove with a stuntperson's sense of space and time, zipping through the DC traffic in his Chevy Cobalt Supercharger while discussing 'narrowband ciphony' and 'electro-political situations'. He talked about launching a hotel into space, the Overlook in orbit. He was also an avid umbraphile. Like Wendy Carlos, Frank chased eclipses, by air and by sea, another vocoder-head seeking totality in the spread spectrum. 'Their greeting traces a moon', spoke Greek electronic composer Lena Platonos through the vocoder, concerning future 'night cities' lit by bioluminescent humans. A couple eats the moon, leaving behind glowing crumbs, then nothing.[27]

Wendy's first photograph of an eclipse was taken in 1963, the year before she first encountered the vocoder in person. She also caught Venus, a tiny glowing dot in the bottom right corner of the frame. The dragon reclears its throat. A reminder. So much to say.

VI. IN MURMURATION

The last solar eclipse seen from Edisto Beach, South Carolina occurred in 2017. Winds from the north have rippled the sandscape, leaving it in a state of furrowed uncertainty. Scientists call it 'accelerated grain beams'. A wrinkle in beach brain, archiving its hydrogeologic past as the dunes erode.

Sanderlings hurry by on important business, racing the tides, their feet in a flicker. Sand percolates. Pelicans skim. A pod of dolphins rises and vanishes just beyond the breakers, dorsal fins cycling. The winter sunset, a pinhole in burnt amber.

Photograph taken by Dave Tompkins, Edisto Island, South Carolina, US, January 2021

I'm at the southern end of the beach on the phone, the vocoder in its chip incarnate. I only hear wind. A flapping IKEA ghost bag interrupts laughter from the other end. Felix Visser, a Dutch vocoder designer/marmalade maker once told me that our voices originate in the wind. They may end there, too. The call is lost. I think of Nixon's presidential limo, how his backseat vocoder accidentally picked up crosstalk from weather satellites.

~~~~~~~~~~~~~~~~~~~~~~~~~~~~

Bell Labs physicist Homer Dudley believed that only the 'gestures' of speech need to be transmitted through the vocoder, signals to be reconstituted at the receiving end. In Frances Scott's film *Valentina* (2020), dancer Valentina Formenti uses her hands while trying to locate Wendy Carlos's memories among her own. She's reciting unpublished excerpts of Wendy's *Playboy* interview, at once lip-syncing and remembering. The vocoder is in phase with her voice, then veers off the map, as if allowing her subconscious to wander, a surrogate for what Wendy wanted to discuss. Eclipses, cartography, physics. You catch glints of speech, words in dissonant bursts of light. Channel overloads could be read as an upwelling of distortion, trying to express feelings yet to be defined or articulated. The work of Wendy's collaborator Rachel Elkind, who is credited with 'articulations' on the soundtrack for *A Clockwork Orange*, often went unnoticed. In *Valentina*, sound designer Chu-Li Shewring's articulations of Valentina are less out of sync than making space for what goes unsaid, a channel in itself.

```
There was
the elaborate
'Biblical
Daydreams': three
interwoven themes
for the prison library
episode, accompanying
Alex's darkly perverted
'olde tyme' fantasies.
The most significant was
'Country Lane', a long
complex cue highlighting
the vocoder, that was
composed for the scene
in which the older
Droogies, now cops,
savagely beat
Alex.
```

Frequencies of speech reach for some totality through passband filters. The vocoder pieces that didn't appear in *A Clockwork Orange* cue Alex's recall of things that both did and didn't happen – fantasy as a dys(topic)function of memory, overdubbed by the memory of Wendy's voice discussing them ('olde tyme'), then layered onto our memory of the film, inhabiting the spaces themselves. The prison library. The 'Country Lane'. The vocoder reconstructing violent 'Biblical Daydreams'.

~~~~~~~~~~~~~~~~~~~~~~~~~~~~

The Russian writer Aleksander Solzhenitsyn once likened vocoder signal processing to demolishing a beach resort into 'bits of matter' and reassembling not the hotels or casinos but the ecology under threat. 'A re-creation of the subtropics, the sound of waves on the shore, the southern air and moonlight.'[28] As if the vocoder's imperfect mapping could be a restoration. Wendy converted this into a spectrogram: a visual representation of the misheard instructional 'how to wreck a nice beach'. How our voices are seen in gatherings of energy around frequency bands and chordal pitch, despite encroachments of granular white noise. She tinkered with the spectrogrammar, refining and articulating its formants. Said she didn't want it to look like a dirty black-and-white *Godzilla* print.[29] She would have preferred her spectrogram to replace the Korg vocoder that appears on the cover of my book, backdropped in sea-foam green.[30]

~~~~~~~~~~~~~~~~~~~~~~~~~~~~~~

The phrase itself, a liminality between what we hear and what we think we hear, is clarified when superimposed upon shorelines no longer recognisable. The erasure too literal, closer still. At Edisto, the bulldozers pushing mountains of sand for dune restoration are the same ones decimating palmetto groves for future rentals. Search 'sandpiper' and you are hit with an onslaught of resorts, condos and roads, as if the birds have been spoken for by developers.[31]

Tufts of foam scoot across the beach like ghosts. I watch sandpipers hunt for fiddler crabs, beaking bubbles. As a collective, these tiny shore birds are referred to as a 'contradiction' or 'timestep'.[32]

In flight, the timestep becomes a murmuration, a collective pulse of acoustic signals and spatial cues. The word itself is defined by the nonverbal, indecipherable to the human ear. It's shaped by what we see, how we take in light – the spectrogram airborne. Less flock than glittering swarm, a bird wave shimmer in black-and-white. Ornithologists liken this winged polyphony to birds playing a game of telephone, against the will of misinformation and signal decay.

The murmuration swerves and dips just above the white caps, formation held, then disappears. In a flash, a reflection. Then again gone, if for a moment.

```
I proposed
composing an
additional work
for the album,
one to precede
Beethoven, and so
'Timesteps' was born.
'Timesteps' featured a
gradual easing-in on
the notion of singing
synthesisers. By the
time they reached the
Ninth Symphony, it
didn't hit them
in the face the
same way.
```

1   Wendy Carlos had already encountered the vocoder in the 1970 film *Colossus: The Forbin Project*: it made its on-screen debut as the voice of a paranoid supercomputer that extorts humanity with nuclear warheads while policing sex and booze consumption. '*The Forbin Project* was the first movie that I recognised for certain used one. By its release, I had my own vocoder. It hit me – the synchronicity – here was an idea whose time had come. Over dinner one evening, I had to give him [Stanley Kubrick] a description of the workings of a typical vocoder.' 1970 also marks the first time a film depicted Bach being played on a Moog: Lewis Stefan Soomil, a UCLA music student from Somalia, plays uncredited in the 1983 documentary *Discovering Electronic Music*.
2   My conversations with Annie Coulter took place between February and May 2021, as well as October 2009.
3   Coulter performs Beethoven's Seventh and the living room goes Bauhaus, morphing into the set of Edgar J. Ulmer's film *The Black Cat* (1934). Ludwig's Second Movement appears in Boris Karloff's monologue at the end: 'Did we not both die here fifteen years ago?' But it's Bela Lugosi who overdubs our memory of the house/set design by Hans Poelzig: 'A masterpiece of construction, built upon the ruins of the masterpiece of deconstruction.'
4   Freff, 'Tuning in to Wendy Carlos', *Electronic Musician Magazine*, November 1986.
5   Dwight W. Batteau and Peter Markey, 'Man/Dolphin Communication: Final Report', 15 December 1966–13 December 1967. See also D. Graham Burnett, *The Sounding of the Whale: Science and Cetaceans in the Twentieth Century*, Chicago: University of Chicago Press, 2012. ('You should see what the dolphins wrote up!' – Mike Vazquez on the nonexistent 'Dolphin/Man Preliminary Report 5000'.)
6   For (dolphin) laughs, listen to the maniac cackle that begins Planet Detroit's *Invasion From Planet Detroit* (Pandisc Records, 1984). Which is not from Detroit but Miami. So again, the dolphins have the first and last laugh.
7   STEAMVALVE: Secure Tactical Electronic Amplitude Modulated Voice Actuated Long-Range Vestigial Emanations. Per Frank Gentges, in his basement in Great Falls, Virginia.
8   Dave Tompkins, *How To Wreck A Nice Beach: The Vocoder From World War II to Hip-Hop*, Chicago: Stop Smiling; Brooklyn: Melville House, 2010, p. 166.
9   B.M. Blackwood and Henry Balfour, 'Ritual and Secular Uses of Vibrating Membranes as Voice Disguisers', *The Journal of the Anthropological Institute of Great Britain and Ireland*, vol.78, no.1/2, 1948, pp.45–69.
10 I've dreamt about my late brother playing Computer World in the Selfish Giant's garden in winter. I've dreamt I had an Auto-Tune retainer grafted to the roof of my mouth with peanut butter rubber cement. It had a tongue-operated pitch control, citing the artificial larynx developed by Gluck et al. in 1921. Nearby a parrot shat on a friend's shoulder and quoted Just-Ice at the wrong speed.
11 My conversation with Ute Holl and Moritz Josch: 'XT vs ET', *ZFM (Zeitschrift fur Medienwissenschaft)*, vol.6, 2012, pp.223–35.
12 Mara Mills, 'Media and Prosthesis: The Vocoder, the Artificial Larynx, and the History of Signal Processing', *Que Parle: Critical Humanities and Social Sciences*, vol.21, no.1, Fall/Winter 2012, pp.107–49.

13 Unused parts of Meg Madsen transcripts courtesy of Delaney Hall for the podcast *99% Invisible*, December 4, 2016.
14 My interview with Don Mehl from my book *How To Wreck A Nice Beach*. A variant of this quote also appears in Mehl's interview with Delaney Hall for *99% Invisible*.
15 On pitch bias, pitch oppression and the gendering of Auto-Tune, see Catherine Provenzano, 'Making Voices: The Gendering of Pitch Correction and the Auto-Tune Effect in Contemporary Pop Music', *Journal of Popular Music Studies*, vol.31, no.2, 2019, pp.63–84.
16 Suzanne Ciani, in my article 'Suzanne Ciani and the Subliminal Property of Being Human', *Paris Review*, 7 August 2017, https://www.theparisreview.org/blog/2017/08/07/as-heard-on-tv/, accessed 4 May 2021.
17 *The David Letterman Show*, August 14, 1980, https://www.youtube.com/watch?v=fZscRHkLMt0, accessed on 3 July 2021.
18 Suzanne Ciani refers to using the vocoder as mapping, placing one sonic filter outline onto another. This could also be a way of hearing and tracing these intersecting histories, when so-called unvoiced sounds transform into the sounds of the unvoiced.
19 I first watched/heard *The Shining* while sitting on my grandad's amber stationary bike. Frame compressed in a Sony TriniTron, a postage stamp of a TV. I pedalled during some of the more terrifying scenes but got looped by Danny's Big Wheel. It (the amber bike) now sits in my mom's den in Charlotte, North Carolina.
20 'I'm trying to fulfill my son's demands for robot music', said my friend A. His son is three and takes his robots seriously. 'I got him into "Man Machine" so I don't have to listen to "Robots" three times in a row.' Apparently he left him in the room dancing to 'Man Machine'. When he returned, the kid was on the Sit N Spin, rotating himself as slowly as possible to match the tempo. I've had this image in a loop ever since. I assume this is what the kid is doing, all the time.
21 Author's correspondence with crypto-historian Craig Bauer, 7 January 2014.
22 Cade Metz, 'There Is A Racial Divide in Speech-Recognition Systems, Researchers Say', *New York Times*, 23 March 2020.
23 Rapper Duane 'Spyder D' Hughes was the first to manipulate the vocoder as a property time share, disguising his voice when making 'The B Beat Classic' for a competing record label, who in turn threatened him with speech analysers. It begins with a vocoded yowl on a pitch bender. As Spyder once told me, he made it 'for all the cats doing acid in Europe'.
24 D. Tompkins, *How To Wreck A Nice Beach*, op. cit., p.255.
25 Teddy Riley in conversation with Jeff Mao, Red Bull Music Academy (RBMA), New York, 5 May 2017.
26 Brigham Young's Language Research Center used the Eltro, the 'information rate exchanger' that voiced HAL's dying 'Daisy' in *2001: A Space Odyssey*, to read excerpts from Antoine de Saint-Exupéry's *The Little Prince* at varying speeds. The study gauged pitch as a function of perceived competence and benevolence when visiting the conceited man's planet.
27 'Their waving signals a moon' is a misremembered Greek-to-vocoder-to-English translation from Lena Platonos's 1980 song 'Gallop':

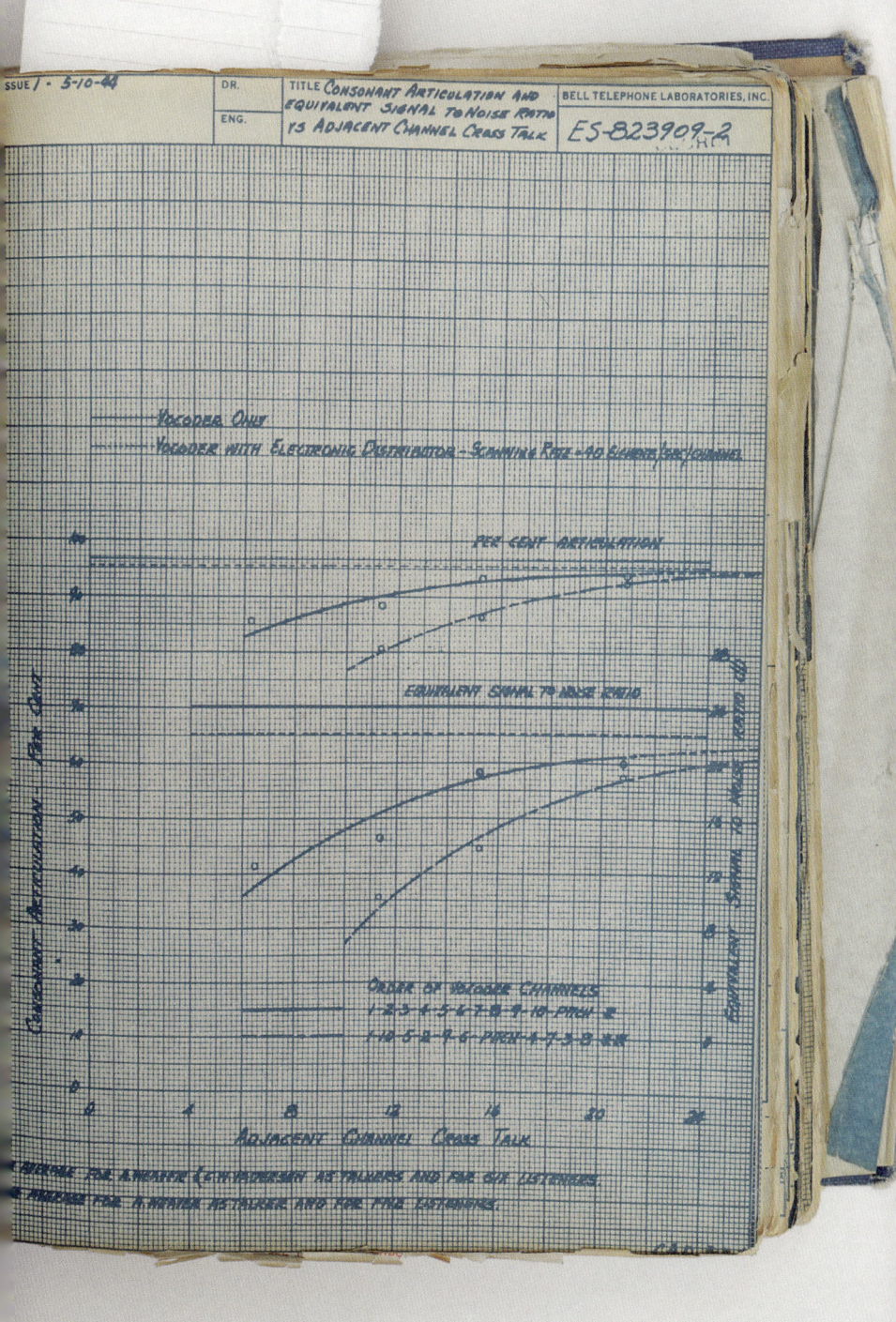

Bell Labs' classified 'secrecy system' vocoder bible (vol. 1, 1932–45). 'Adjacent Channel Cross Talk' diagram

'Their greeting traces a moon / and as they move closer to each other / they are connected from the same gallop of the first rain / the colour of the moon from their contact'.

28 Aleksander Solzhenitsyn, *The First Circle*, trans. Thomas P. Whitney, Evanston: Northwestern University Press, 1997, p.50.
29 My correspondence with Wendy Carlos concerning her generous contribution to *How To Wreck A Nice Beach*.
30 See *How To Wreck A Nice Beach*, *op. cit.*
31 For a strange tumble down dune oblivion, I recommend *The Shout* (1978), which frequented my conversations with Frances Scott over the past year while she worked on *Incantation, Wendy*. Set on the North Devon coast, *The Shout* has the most terrifying sound ever captured on film, according to the British Film Institute (BFI). Six out of six bystanding sheep would've agreed but couldn't because they'd been shouted dead. Alan Bates suffers from an aborigine curse that allows him to fatally bellow anyone within earshot. John Hurt is a sound designer who howls into a vocoder. Suzanne York plays Hurt's wife, tired of Hurt and seduced by Bates. The film is framed in Bates's retelling from inside a scorekeeper's booth at a cricket match that takes place at a mental health hospital. Did any of this actually happen?
32 For revenge, search 'birdshit vocoder' in YouTube and you'll land on a vocoded meditation concerning an overnight bombirdment of parked cars and SUVs. *These birds, they shitted up a storm out here. Literally!*

All Orbit quotes are from interviews with Wendy Carlos that appeared in my book *How To Wreck A Nice Beach*. Wendy was in the early stages of writing 'Timesteps' when she started reading Anthony Burgess's novel *A Clockwork Orange*, published in 1962, as if envisioning the soundtrack before the film was made. As Wendy says, it was an 'autonomous composition with an uncanny affinity for *Clockwork*.'

rehearsal letter

Tom Richards with Frances Scott

On the following pages, sections from Wendy Carlos's original scores for 'Timesteps' and 'Theme from A Clockwork Orange (Beethovania)' (1971) have been reinterpreted by musician and instrument designer Tom Richards using the Mini Oramics machine. The Mini Oramics is based on an original 1976 design by British composer and inventor Daphne Oram and was realised by Richards in 2016. It is a musical interface that allows the composer to draw graphic scores on clear-film overhead projector rolls, which are then read directly by the machine, creating 'drawn sound synthesis'.

These scores have been made as part of the soundtrack development for *Wendy*. They have been presented in two iterations, first as a live event at TACO! in 2019, and then as *rehearsal letter*, a recorded studio session by Tom Richards and Frances Scott for transmediale x CTM 2021 in Berlin. A 'rehearsal letter' is a letter of the alphabet used at structural points in an orchestral score, to indicate where a musician or performer might begin, if not at the start. In this spirit, the session presents fragments of a score in the process of its construction.

Scores accompanied by extracts from Frances Scott and Tom Richards's conversation with Ben Evans James (transmediale) and Christine Kakaire (CTM), published online for transmediale 2021–22 in the *Almanac for Refusal*, which is updated every full moon over the course of a year.

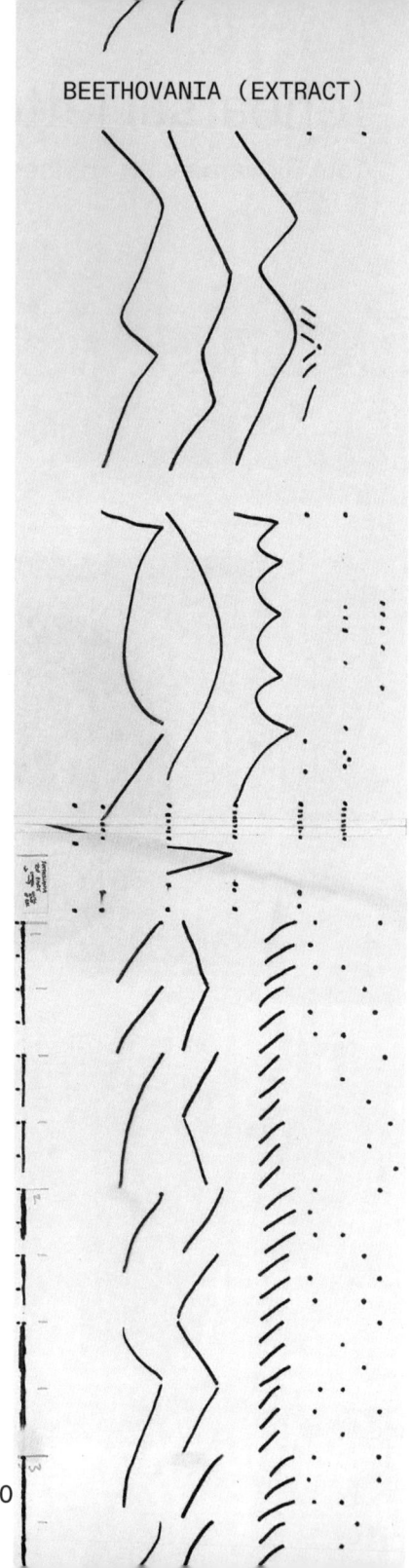

BEETHOVANIA (EXTRACT)

Tom Richards

TIMESTEPS • (EXTRACT)

We will be recording more music and sound for *Wendy*. Frances is also working with sound designer Chu-Li Shewring, so I'm looking forward to seeing what they do with the audio stems we have so far. For this recording, we brought together the Mini Oramics with hand-made modular synths, modified turntables with custom dub-plates, another sequencer and an analogue vocoder. 'Timesteps' is a really challenging piece. I'm not trying to make a faithful copy, I am attempting to make something new from the process of trying to understand and digest Carlos's music — keeping it quite open. As a relatively untrained, self-taught musician, this is a real learning curve! The other piece of music, 'Beethovania', is a more faithful rendition, and we've used this to top and tail the session with the 'Timesteps' inspired pieces forming three movements in the middle.

This kind of intuitive interpretation also makes me think about Carlos and Oram both having a vision for electronic music in their early careers, which didn't fit with the academic trends of the 1960s. They saw the potential for electronic sounds to be expressive and humanistic, which went against the grain of the fashionable mathematical approaches of the serialist and aleatoric schools, both of which are closely related to the early experiments in computer music. Oram called these approaches 'music by slide rule' and went on to create her expressive 'drawn sound' synthesiser, Oramics. Carlos made *Switched-On Bach* (1968), which popularised electronic music and was a pivotal step in expanding its realms beyond academia. That said, I don't think my collaboration with Frances and the subsequent linking of our research was prescribed or particularly deliberate in terms of the Carlos/Oram link. Frances and I were introduced by a mutual friend, Mat Jenner, who thought we had similar interests, and the collaboration was quite organic. In this context, we are two artists experimenting and trying things out; it's more about capturing an essence or finding a non-verbal way to describe these subjects. Carlos and Oram have both been subjected to a lot of hyperbole and pigeonholing in the media, when both are really complex, multifaceted individuals. I think we are trying to explore their characters through their creative outputs, outside of any labels or preconceived notions.

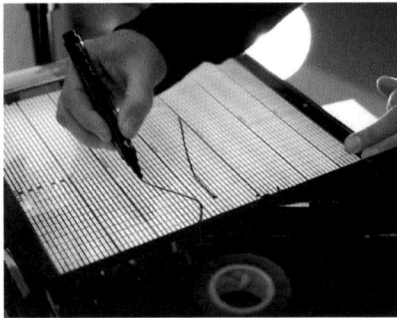

Frances Scott For the film, Tom began the interpretation of 'Beethovania', and I filmed a couple of rolls of 16mm on a hand-wound Bolex. There's a pulsing quality to the image and, because of the way it's hand-processed, you get inconsistencies and occasional forms flashing in a frame that seem to be synchronous with the drawn shapes on acetate moving across the light bed. With analogue film you work at a different pace, it allows you to think differently and deliberately about how you capture images. This is partly because there's a delay, not an immediate result, and the expense of shooting analogue film and even the heaviness of the camera means you don't film everything. I like this time as a buffer, time to think! I somehow see this time being part of Tom's process too, and there's a similar component of not totally knowing what the outcome will be. There's also a nice connection between the drawing on a film-like substrate, in Oram's early experiments actually on 35mm, and 'cameraless' filmmaking, where images are generated by processes like painting onto or scratching into the emulsion, collage or direct exposure of the photosensitive layer.

Tom Richards   I've also worked with analogue film, both as an artist and as a technician and projectionist. I love the physicality of the medium, and it feels very natural to now be working with sound in a similar fashion with the Mini Oramics. To be drawing on film to score a film is a pretty unique experience these days. With Mini Oramics the 'performance' is in the drawing, which you generally do in advance of playback and recording. This process can be painstaking and sometimes hit-or-miss. Imagine trying to draw the correct vibrato graph or the volume envelope of a single note — things that are normally looked after by the instrument you are playing or by intuition and improvisation in real-time. Mini Oramics is not like that: you have to conceive every parameter of every note as a drawing or graph and then get them all to work together. On the other hand, each and every note can have a very precise timbral and dynamic character if you want it to. This is exactly what Oram wanted for her interface, to be able to compose this level of nuance. In terms of restrictions and freedoms of gestures, you can't really draw something 'wrong' on the Mini Oramics, any drawing will make a sound, but it does have its own syntax and graphic code. You need to understand a bit about how it works to be able to predict the outcome of any given gesture, and more loosely, keeping each gesture within its given parameter channel will help contain the chaos.

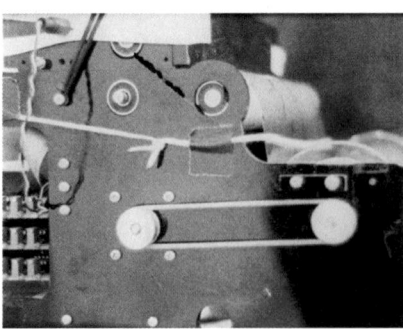

Frances Scott Most of Tom's drawing happened before we made the recording, although some of the earlier 16mm film was shot as he was scoring the work. I especially like the process of his enacting and re-enacting, drawing and erasing. Looking through the lens, you're also aware of Tom teasing the score through, rewinding and slowing down, in the moments where he plays the instrument by hand rather than its being automated. You can hear this hand-wound section in the 'warm-up' to 'Beethovania', towards the end of *rehearsal letter*. We tried to capture this, his touch, but also how he appears and disappears, a partly seen figure, making the Mini Oramics seem to have a life of its own.

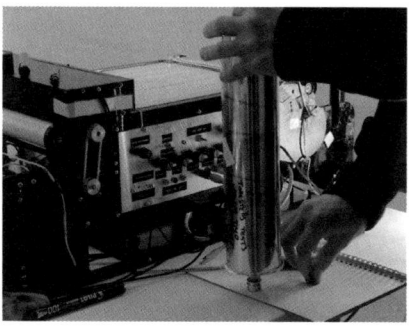

Throughout: Sections of score and film stills from Tom Richards and Frances Scott, *rehearsal letter*, 2021

'Thunder egg' agate found at Thunder Bay, Ontario by the artist's grandparents. On 10 June 2021, Thunder Bay was in the path of annularity for the solar eclipse.

Contributors

Frances Scott is an artist working with the moving image. Her film work, informed by a collaborative and research-led process, takes multiple forms, from exhibitions to installations, screenings, events, broadcasts and publications, including recent presentations at: 67. International Short Film Festival Oberhausen (distributor screening); Rencontres Internationales Paris/Berlin; transmediale x CTM, Berlin; TACO!, London; 57th New York Film Festival; LIAF, Close Up Film Centre, London; Het Bos, Antwerp; The Bower, London; Tate St Ives, Cornwall; Whitechapel Gallery, London; Yorkshire Sculpture Park and Art Licks; South West Film and Television Archive, Plymouth; and Focal Point Gallery, Southend. She is a recipient of the Stuart Croft Foundation Moving Image Award (2017) and her films are distributed by LUX.

Beth Bramich is a writer and editor based in London. Her writing has featured in *Art Monthly*, *Frieze* and *Afterall*, and she regularly collaborates with artists on films, exhibitions, events and publications. In 2019 she joined the working group for the 'Feminist Duration Reading Group', co-organising an ongoing programme of workshops and discussions. She teaches at Central Saint Martins, University of the Arts London, and is currently developing a research project into feminist film collectives formed in the 1970s in the UK and Australia, and their contemporary legacies.

Chu-Li Shewring is a filmmaker and sound designer collaborating with directors and artists on documentaries, short films and features for television, cinema and gallery contexts. She has worked as a sound designer on Steve McQueen's *Hunger* (2008) and with artists including Beatrice Gibson, Ben Rivers, Jeremy Deller, Patrick Keiller, Phil Coy, Siobhan Davies and David Hinton. Her sound credits include award-winning projects at Sundance Film Festival, BAFTA and Cannes Film Festival. She has worked with Frances Scott since *CANWEYE { }* (2016). Her film works are co-directed with writer/director Adam Gutch, including screenings at Channel 4; BFI London Film Festival; International Film Festival Rotterdam; and Images Festival, Toronto. In 2017, she was awarded the Jules Wright Prize for her sound work in film.

Phil Coy is an artist and filmmaker. He collages concepts rooted in the radical art and literature of the twentieth century, with languages and architectures of contemporary global commerce. Recent exhibitions and screenings include: South London Gallery; Eastside Projects, Birmingham; Ferens Art Gallery and Maritime Museum, Hull; FACT,

Liverpool; BFI London Film Festival; Focal Point Gallery, Southend; and Whitechapel Gallery, London. He was Leverhulme artist in residence at Rutherford Appleton Laboratory, and his new public work Stereo Pair was installed at Brunel University in 2021. He is currently working on a commission for Matt's Gallery to coincide with the launch of their new space in Nine Elms, London in 2021.

Juliet Jacques is a writer, filmmaker, academic and broadcaster. Her books include *Trans: A Memoir* (Verso, 2015), based on her *Transgender Journey* series for *The Guardian* (2010–12), and *Variations* (Influx Press, 2021), a collection of short stories exploring the history of trans and non-binary people in the UK. Her short fiction, essays and journalism have appeared in numerous publications, including *Art Review*, *Frieze*, *Granta*, *The New York Times*, *Sight & Sound*, *Time Out* and *Wire*, and her short films have been screened in galleries and festivals worldwide. She hosts the arts radio programme *Suite (212)* on Resonance 104.4fm and teaches at the Royal College of Art, London and elsewhere.

Valentina Formenti started her career as a dancer training at the London Contemporary Dance School. Since graduating in 1994, she has been working as a performer, co-creator and rehearsal director with many dance companies and directors, across theatre, opera and film, including Requardt & Rosenberg, New Adventures, The Cholmondeleys, Fevered Sleep, Simon Vincenzi, Fabulous Beast, Vincent Dance Theatre, Sasha Milavic Davies, Made in China and Paramount Pictures. Her interest in film has seen her develop a parallel career as a freelance camera operator, specialising in the capture of live performance. Since 2006 she has been an in-house camera operator/director at The Place Theatre, London.

Stine Hebert is an independent curator and art historian based in Copenhagen. She has curated exhibitions for various spaces internationally and taught at universities and art academies in Europe. She has previously held positions as curator at Kunsthal Charlottenborg, curator at Malmö Art Museum, acting director of BAC – Baltic Art Center and rector of Funen Art Academy. Most recently she was dean of the Academy of Fine Art at Oslo National Academy of the Arts. She has curated exhibitions at institutions including Kunsthal Charlottenborg, Copenhagen; Malmö Art Museum; Tate Modern, London.

Dave Tompkins is a writer currently working on a book about Miami Bass (Simon & Schuster, 2022). His first book, *How To Wreck A Nice Beach: The Vocoder From World War II to Hip-Hop*, was published by

StopSmiling/Melville House. He has written for *The Paris Review*, *The New Yorker*, *New York Magazine*, *The Wire* and *Ego Trip*. He recently contributed to the *Unsound Intermission* anthology ("It Takes A Cavitation of Millions") and wrote about the Jungle Brothers and dowsing ("Done By the Trickle Trickle") for the forthcoming collection, *Boogie Down Predictions*, edited by Roy Christopher, to be published by Strange Attractor/MIT Press. Born in North Carolina, he lives in Brooklyn.

Tom Richards is a London-based composer and instrument designer, who works in the overlap between sound art, sculpture and music. For his PhD at Goldsmiths, Richards researched the work of Daphne Oram, culminating in a functional build of Mini Oramics, which the British electronic music pioneer conceptualised over forty years ago but never realised during her lifetime: a machine that can translate drawings into sound and compositions. Richards's own output often features textured, evolving, polyrhythmic improvisations. He has performed and shown works throughout the UK, including Tate Britain and the Queen Elizabeth Hall, and in the United States, Germany, Peru, Japan and Sweden.

Wendy Carlos can be read in her own words – including access to interviews, photographs and resources – at wendycarlos.com

An Endless Supply is a design studio in Birmingham, UK, established in 2011 by Harry Blackett and Robin Kirkham. They work with artists and organisations making websites and printed matter. Bobo is the irregular publishing arm of AES, and was launched in 2019. AES and Frances Scott have worked together since 2017, when they designed the printed script for her film ~~Its soil was a plot~~ *she do the tree in different voices*, and the titles for her films, *Valentina* (2020) and forthcoming *Wendy* (2022).

TACO! is an artist-led space for research, production and exchange located in Thamesmead, South East London. TACO! is engaged with its local context and centres the work and role of artists in all the work it undertakes, supporting a dialogue between artists, audiences, community and place. Activities are experimental and collaborative, presented through a public programme that includes exhibitions, events, discussions, workshops, screenings, publishing and co-authored participatory projects with local people and groups. TACO! currently comprises a gallery, bookshop and broadcast studio for RTM.FM, a community radio station.

Image credits

All images courtesy Frances Scott unless otherwise specified.

pp.8–9, 14, 33 Peabody and the Thamesmead Community Archive
pp.16–17 Fenollosa-Weld Collection, 11.4584. Courtesy the Museum of Fine Arts Boston.
p.18 Tom Richards
p.19 Prelinger Library
p.25 Beth Bramich
pp.38–39 Courtesy David Pearson and the BBC. The five-part series, *A Change of Sex*, is available to view on BBC iPlayer from 3 June 2021
p.67 The Royal Astronomical Society
p.70 Annie Coulter
p.72 Courtesy Pitt Rivers Museum, University of Oxford (1931.46.1)
pp.73, 82 Dave Tompkins
p.74 AT&T Archives and History Center
pp.75, 87 Courtesy Ralph LaRue Miller, photographs by Kate Glicksberg
p.76 The Pritzker Military Museum & Library
pp.90–95 Tom Richards and Frances Scott

Acknowledgements

Incantation, Wendy is part of *Wendy*, a research residency and commission with TACO!. Supported by Arts Council England, Peabody and An Endless Supply.

rehearsal letter was commissioned as a live studio session for transmediale x CTM 2021, Berlin.

Diviner was made for the Peninsula Arts Film Commission, a partnership between Peninsula Arts at Plymouth University; the South West Film and Television Archive; and The Box, Plymouth.

Frances Scott would like to thank Fabio Altamura, Natasha Bird, Will Brady, Beth Bramich, Phil Coy, Nicholas Crowe, Michael Curran, Lisa Drew, Ben Evans-James, Valentina Formenti, Sandra Gorel, Bea Haut, Stine Hebert, Juliet Jacques, Mat Jenner, Robin Kirkham, Emily LaBarge, Emma Leach, Adriana Marques, Andrea Martinez, Deirdre O'Dwyer, Ragnhild Olsen, Nora O Murchú, David Pearson, Sian Prosser, Tom Richards, Emma Richardson, Jesse de Rocquigny, Jan Rohlf, Christine Scott, Fiona Scott, Chu-Li Shewring, Dani Tagen, Dave Tompkins, Simon Vincenzi and Thom Walker.

Dave Tompkins would like to thank Wendy Carlos, Josh Cheon, Chris Corwin, Kate Glicksberg, Sheldon Hochheiser, Julius Kammerl, Dorothy Madsen, Lena Platonos, Brian Sears and Will Stephenson.

Stine Hebert would like to thank MC Coble for guidance and insights.

Incantation, Wendy
Frances Scott

Edited by Beth Bramich

Copy Editor Deirdre O'Dwyer
Research Assistant Thom Walker

Designed by An Endless Supply
Typeset in Diatype, Diatype Mono and Media 77
Reprographics by DL Imaging
Printed by Aldgate Press, London
on Arena Natural Smooth 90gsm, 300gsm

© Frances Scott and contributors, 2021

Published by Bobo

Bobo, Unit 3, Minerva Works
158 Fazeley Street, Birmingham B5 5RT
bobobooks.org

All rights reserved. Apart from fair dealing for the purposes of private study, research, criticism or reviews as permitted under the Copyright Act, no part of this publication may be reproduced in any form without permission in writing from the publisher.

Every effort has been made to trace copyright holders and to obtain their permission for the use of copyright material. The publisher apologises for any errors or omissions and would be grateful if notified of any corrections that should be incorporated in future reprints or editions of this book.

ISBN 978-1-9160775-1-5